REVOLUTION ON CANVAS

EDITED BY RICH BALLING

AD ASTRA BOOKS • CALIFORNIA

REVOLUTION ON CANVAS

Editor: Rich Balling
Associate Editors: Chris Haynie, Charles Adams & Vanessa Chibba

Published by Ad Astra Books
Ad Astra Books / PO BOX 2938 / Orange, Ca 92859
www.adastrabooks.com / info@adastrabooks.com

Cover Image: Matthew Lessner
Cover Design: Marc McKnight
Layout: Michael Hain

ISBN 0-9747316-0-9

Printed In Canada
Hignell Book Printing
488 Burnell Street
Winnipeg, Manitoba R3G 2B4

For Charlene Rogers

"one of these days, I'll learn from my mistakes
and not rush to opinions before I have given
works in any medium
the time and full attention they deserve."

—Gerald Locklin
from "lars jansson: ballads"

TABLE OF CONTENTS

INTRODUCTION

FOREWORD

INTRODUCTION- If you're reading this book, you've probably seen them—in a library or a bookstore or on a subway—posters of Shaquille O'Neal or Cameron Diaz or Al Gore (holding favorite books) and telling you to do one thing: Read! Somberly clad actors on the big three networks say the same thing. And so does my 17-month-old son (about 219 times a day)—"Read, read, read, Da Da!" And so I do. He crawls in my lap and off we go into lands of primary colors and levitating fruit and numbers dressed like people and farm animals. It's not sophisticated stuff. He's not yet ready for Hamlet or Camus or even a standard-issue Grisham novel. But by reading these little books now (these books whose A-B rhymes invade my sleep and whose monosyllabic words cloud my lectures at school), someday he will be. Admittedly, I am lucky. I was brought up with books, frequently read to, taught to read well by both teachers and my parents. My son will have the same luck as Shaq and Cameron and Mr. Gore and me. So the statistics say. Reading parents produce reading children.

I am always deeply affected—saddened mostly—that so many of my students come from homes where there are no books. Most of them will attest to this, when asked, without hesitating—some of them, oddly, with a bit of bravado. Unfortunately, it's no wonder that these students are the ones who struggle with even basic writing. It's no wonder that the source of their struggles (those with learning disabilities not withstanding) is of course the lack of exposure to reading materials, and often reading parents, at home. Obviously, the students to whom I refer here have at least basic literacy skills or they wouldn't be able to survive even the first semester of college. Of course there are those far worse off than those who can eke out a C- in freshman or even remedial composition.

So what about those who can't read a sentence? How can they be helped? And who will help them? There are innumerable reasons—individual and systemic—for illiteracy and weak reading and writing skills. Economic issues of course come to everyone's mind first. How can a child learn to read and appreciate books if there is no money for books and no one to take the child to the library or to sit with him and sound out the word "ca, ca, carrot" or "butterfly"? Many parents are simply not available because of second (and third and fourth) jobs. This combined with the simple fact that many parents can't read well themselves makes the origins of illiteracy far less mysterious. Illiteracy, like poverty, is hereditary.

But there is hope and help. And there are people who care. The musicians whose ideas and words that are featured in this wonderful book are committed to making people aware of the problem of illiteracy in the United States and of the programs available to combat illiteracy. Programs like the National Center for Family Literacy (famlit.org), to whom the proceeds of this book will be donated, succeed in improving the literacy skills of both kids and their parents by bringing them together in a supportive environment and teaching them side by side, so that they learn together, improve together, and encourage each other to work toward a common goal—the goal of making their family a literate one. How beautiful.

John Payne
Associate Professor of English, Cypress College

FOREWORD - When I first heard Dead Kennedys' "Too Drunk to Fuck," I thought, "This is great! Someone using the F-word in a song." I remember slam dancing around my government-subsidized apartment punching holes in the walls. It was the next best thing to saying, "fuck you" to your boss, your teachers, hell, even to your parents. At the time I didn't even know the complete meaning of the song, I was hooked on the fact that the catchy chorus kept repeating the word fuck (it wasn't your average pop radio love song). On closer inspection, I became more aware of the sarcasm and irony in the lyrics. It was a frat boy chant denouncing stereotypical frat boy behavior. I had a Punk Rock epiphany.

I thought to myself, after years of AC/DC and Rush, there was finally music with a lyrical content that went beyond telling stories about fantasy worlds, and bar room bravado. I wanted to hear more. Instead of getting "shook all night long," my brain and value system got a wake up call. These Punk Rock poets were speaking out about the ills of government, the shortcomings of a Napoleon complex and the hierarchy of economic classes in our nation's capital. I learned about politics, psychology and sociology by reading the lyrics of Jello Biafra, Ian MacKaye, and Steve Polcari from Marginal Man. Here were prophetic, pro-active speakers using music as a tool for change.

Twenty years later, the values that I learned about growing up in the D.C. scene still hold true. Actions speak louder than words, but it was those words that inspired action. Too many bands out there underestimate the influence their lyrics have on people, and that irony can be a double-edged sword. Responsibility is literally in your hand.

Rusty Pistachio
H2O

In an attempt to preserve the integrity of the work, we have chosen to leave the text as it was when we received it. It's not our business to decide who meant what where, and we don't want to insult anyone with blanket editing that might sacrifice what was meant by the work in its original form, whether it be on a type-written page, or a drink-stained napkin.

WILLIAM E. BECKETT
The Academy

Realization.
Enter The Author.
Home. Security. Illusion. Ego. Self. Lust. Blame. Sloth.
Betrayal and Fear.
Enter Panic.
Journey. Road. Quest. Reflect. Chaos. Discover. Condemn.
Adjust and Change.

The search has begun. This is Page One.
Men meet your maker, I give you "The Author".
He may look familiar because he looks like your mirror.
You've lied like a lawyer, but don't deny it when you're
face to face with demons dancing off of mirror images
reflecting all that you wanted. So far from perfect.
Enter The Mirror.

Onward, we will strive for betterment.
Take it for what it's worth, this truth that you've realized.
You're not who you thought you were, it's time you see the
other side of
what   you   have   become...   Nothing but
Single serving selfish chapters of sacrificial moral standards.
No stranger to apathy in Bold situations. Take your time to
make it happen.
Bring your mirror, and spare your excuse for a self-serving
mystery.
This is a drastic endeavor. Desperate times call for desperate
measures.

Take it, or leave it, if you will.
From this point on, it's Courtrooms and Battlefields.
The way you thought it would all work out... we've hit
Autumn.
Just follow the storyboard. The Fall of The Author.
From this point on, it's Exposure and Recovery.
take it, or leave it, if you will.

Exit The Author.

JARROD TAYLOR
In Reverent Fear

THE SPOKES OF A NEW TYRANY

we've set our mark upon the baron shade we've made,
with the taste of our mistakes and the heat of our decrees.
the broken sped throughout into the air of distant plains,
i'm holding up your prudence and betting further dares.

still rusty with subjection and fruitful in our march,
you're downstairs and i'm here spinning clever fate in the dark.
with the hate in your remarks when you've spoken only love,
i'm praying for health and you're praying from above.

so we danced and we laughed at the normalcy of good fortune,
her eyes ever glowing in sickness and in health.
with focus and chemistry we took the world alive,
sorting through musings of a life i cannot provide.
she's in love with ideas i'm in love when she cries,
her neck gently bending and shaping the night.
the morning is begging us awake yet holding softer,
she's the taste of a millionaire, and i've the wallet of a pauper.

JARROD TAYLOR
In Reverent Fear

THE BUTCHER/THE BARBER

Cinnamon glowing the vices that I want to be bound to. The
calming breaking down the rain on the asphalt. Wet with
fever like I'm missing the better. And I know this is just the
beginning. Still I wait, with suitcase.
With the math of you and I aside...it's the skin on your
jawbone, woven into you. One more pausing silence. Two
dimes on your eyelids. Third time's a charm, and the fourth
time is too far. I adore mi amor. I am the patron shaking
and you're only dreamed. Pure and Golden, here are gifts
from the thousands before. To HEAR the voice of the angels,
"Raise anew!"
I'm recovered because you're warm in truth. Still I wait,
with suitcase.
With the math of you and I aside...it's the skin on your
jawbone woven into you. You are my serenity, when I think
of you, I forget to breathe.

NATE BARCALOW
Finch

Veins coarse, wet, abrasive. Dimwitted
Happiness
On and on about the neverminds of Me
Scratch your bloody itch-

This is The Tourniquet-
One more for Innocence, with a sad face
Looking at this...
Well, what's left of It.

Never a dull moment
A Lonely Desert Night to build a Fire
Warm this abandoned meat-
Reckless and ignorant

A Victim of black and white.

COLIN FRANGICETTO
This Day Forward

WHAT IT MEANS TO TRAVEL THE STRAIGHTEST
LINE:

placed, so out of focus
somehow i find myself inside the frame
within this concrete empire
i
swear
to
leave
stand and absorb all the scapes of the land
stare harder, with intentions of figuring it all out
and then held for ransom,
who would make this trade?
the blurring rails and power plants
have me thinking that ive lost the way.

DAN ARNOLD
A Static Lullaby

...Of course I hear you!
You're the taste upon my lips when I wake.
Sometimes you're the only faith I have.
Searching...always searching for more.
I'm enslaved by you, but you make me feel as free as can be.
I want to touch you.
I'll catch your scent on the air and my feet don't
stop, they can't stop! We must keep dancing in your name!

M U S I C
The only air I breathe.

JEREMY TALLEY
The Bled

PERFECT TEETH

i taste your wife your kids your new car.
accessories.
i taste your game show grin. your perfect teeth.
i reach and miss. i spit at ceiling fans and sundowns.
your name under my pillow. your eyelash on my lips.
make a wish.
you sold me everything.
i taste your new home in flames.
i taste your calloused typewriter paws.
oh so television.
success.
your secretary is the mistress i never had.
glowing.
i smell your teenage daughter's tears.
she reeks of sedatives.
i need this.
i try to become you.
anything to escape this sk(prison)in.

JONATHON NEWBY
Brazil

YOUR NAME AGAIN?

ok
you just walked out the door with the won't-ever-happen-again
ok
it was supposedly *incommunicado*
ok
not that I'm jealous or upset or feel strange in any way
well... ok

JONATHON NEWBY
Brazil

A POEM ABOUT LOVE AND HATE IN THE
INFORMATION AGE

10010111000101101001
1001001010101010001101010
1010010110LOVE101001001
100101011010010010101001
110100101001010101010
0101100101HATE0101001010
01001010010101001010.

JONATHON NEWBY
Brazil

LOGIC

Four commuters are riding in a train car. One gets up to use
the restroom. Upon his return he finds another passenger
has taken his seat. The woman next to the passenger that
took the first passenger's seat is wearing a red overcoat. The
man across from the woman wearing the red overcoat is not
the passenger carrying the briefcase. The man with the
briefcase was there from the beginning and has not moved.
Seconds later they were all killed when the train derailed.

JONATHON NEWBY
Brazil

THREE HAIKUS

irony of chance
on the corpse of truth I dance
bitter end romance

*   *   *

honestly I'm not
nothing happens fast enough
words confuse the thought

*   *   *

seconds tick away
the illusion starts to fray
je suis desole

GABE SAPORTA
Midtown

THE TRAGEDY OF THE HUMAN CONDITION

I'm still waiting for the news dad,
That she's gone and never coming back.
I can't go on because the strength I had is gone
And I find it hard to get out of bed

Oh yeah, don't you know it's true son,
You can't really know someone.
Even though we sleep together we're alone
And I find it hard to get out of bed

And we operate but
I still feel alone
And I can't complain
Cause she's so beautiful
Yes we all have made mistakes

GABE SAPORTA
Midtown

Everyday the same joke
I never think it's funny
Nothing's ever what it seems
The truth becomes a dream

And we reach for what we're missing in ourselves

I fought away this desperation
I made attempts to quell temptation
I swear to god I tried, but we could never compromise
You could never change me

And we reach for what we're missing in—
We don't know how to let love in
Don't you cry
For me
Because I'm already dead.

BOBBY DARLING
Gatsby's American Dream

INDUSTRY, THE AGE OF DINOSAURS, AND THE END OF CIVILIZATION

they call this the badland's baby
but it used to be bayou
the shore of an inland sea
and i can still hear you coming
what foul beast stalks this way
the night is dim
but i catch the scent of your arrogance
as you rear your head i can see your eyes gleaming
catching light from the moon
like a pair of knives
to cut me down
yeah there is a hole in the world
and the light is leaking out
spilling like water
and i can still hear you coming
what new devilry is this?
i saw you rise
and creep across the sky
and all night as i fled
you came behind
eating all the stars
we dig to find
why the light left
skulls and bone
rock and stone
whisper stories
tales of glory
and a tragic fall from grace
we're still falling
just like the dinosaurs
what makes you think we'll end up any different

Summer Songs 1995 ©

JOSEPH KARAM
The Locust

WET DREAM WAR MACHINE

Stop talking politics
Rephrase, Rephrase
Hibernating phantom friend
Witness, Witness

There's a hotbed of isms around here.

All hail the chopper,
the blitzkrieg,
the tank.
Never mind the ethics involved.

Stop talking politics.
Calculate, Eliminate
Witness, This mess

Who's got their nightmare glasses?
It's time to go driving.
Prime time is
crime time is
nuclear might.

All hail the chopper,
the blitzkrieg,
the tank.
Never mind the ethics involved.

SHANE TOLD
Silverstein

BLEEDS NO MORE

My heart bleeds no more; now, it's been turned to stone. Your stomach feels sick for someone else. I've broken both my legs falling for you. Drag me on the ground. Powerless I stand, tarnished blade, cutting through, pushed into my vein. Blood still stains my hands. Sharpening my sense of pain outside, my heart bleeds no more. Killing everything off inside. Make sense of everything you tried to hide from me. My heart bleeds no more; now, it's been turned to stone. My stomach feels sore from cutting up. I ruined all my sanctity for you. Smash me on the ground. I wanted to convince myself there's nothing else to do. I wanted to provide you with proof of what you put me through. I wanted to pretend that I was you.

MIKE BURKETT
NOFX

RE-GAINING UNCONSCIOUSNESS

First they put away the dealers, keep our kids safe and off the
street
Then they put away the prostitutes, keep married men
cloistered at home
Then they shooed away the bums, then they beat and bashed
the queers
Turned away asylum seekers, fed us suspicions and fears
We didn't raise our voice, we didn't make a fuss
It's funny there was no one left to notice when they came for
us

Looks like witches are in season, you better fly your flag and
be aware
Of anyone who might fit the description, diversity is now our
biggest fear
Now with our conversations tapped and our differences
exposed
How ya supposed to love your neighbor, without minds and
curtains closed
We used to worry about big brother, now we got a big father
and an even bigger mother

And you still believe, this aristocracy gives a fuck about you
They put the mock, in demockracy and you swallowed every
hook
The sad truth is you would rather follow the school into the
net
Cuz swimming alone at sea is not the kind of freedom you
actually want
So go back to your crib and suck on a tit and go bask the
warmth of your diaper
You're sitting in shit and piss while sucking a huge pacifier a
country of adult infants
A legion of mental midgets a country of adult infants a
country of adult infants
All re-gaining their unconsciousness

MIKE BURKETT
NOFX

IDIOTS ARE TAKING OVER

It's not the right time to be sober now the idiots are taking
over
Spreading like a social cancer is there an answer

Mensa membership conceding, tell me why (And how) are all
the stupid people breeding
Watson, it's really elementary, the industrial revolution has
flipped a bitch on evolution
The benevolent and wise are being thwarted, ostracized, what
a bummer
The world keeps getting dumber insensitivity is standard, and
faith is being fancied over reason

Darwin's rolling over in his coffin, cuz the fittest are
surviving much less often
Now everything seems to be reversing, and it's worsening
Someone flopped a steamer in the gene pool
Now angry mob mentality is no longer the exception, it's the
rule
And I'm starting to feel a lot like Charlton Heston, stranded
on a primate planet
Apes and orangutans that ran it to the ground, were generals
and the armies who obeyed them
Followers following fables, philosophies that enable them to
rule without regard
It sounds all too familiar

There's no point for democracy when ignorance is celebrated
Political scientists get the same one vote as some Arkansas
inbred
Majority rule don't work in the mental institutions
Sometimes the smallest, softest voice carries the grand
biggest solutions

So what are we left with? a nation of god fearing pregnant nationalists
Who feel it's their duty to populate their homeland
Pass on traditions, how to get ahead religions and prosperity via simpleton culture
The idiots are taking over.

ST. ANTHONY

I'm sure the mist of an invisible spring
    must have invaded the young Ascetic's mind.
            FORNICATION,

The last temptation carrying secret baskets
    filled with the miniature gardens of Persian kings.

    How was it that the painter Heronomous Bosch
    kept his hands still to paint that Dutch mistress
    hiding half of her flesh behind a corroded tree trunk.
This royal lady of unchastity,
    promising nurture and sweetness
to all of her loyal subjects.

    I've crowned her queen fornication of North Africa.
    The woman who roams the World putting plastic
    Lilies behind the ears of lonely men.

Saint Anthony must have heard her soft seductive sound
in the desert.
Fornication's silk mantle blowing in the dry wind.
That savoring sound of pleasure
Then the voice:
    " Do not deny what is good for you, stupid Egyptian.
    Do not deny what is natural."

I imagine the young Saint closing his eyes and trying
to transform his racing heart of blood and body
into an illumined Lily that would fill his entire
being with a living scent.

VINCENT REYES
Friends In The Mountains

WATCHING TRAFFIC FROM THE NAVEL OF A
GOLDEN LOTUS

*"If one speaks or acts with wicked mind, because of that, pain pursues
him, even as a wheel follows the hoof of the draught ox."*
                                        -The Dhammapada

A lady crying in traffic gave the day the eternity it was
looking for.

            The steering wheel,
                rusted under her tears,
                        became the sun.

            A miracle or alchemy?
                An armillary sphere

            Like the Buddhist wheel of truth I had seen
            in some museum's private collection,
        placed behind glass and an alarm system.

            I remember the back of her head,
Mother of this family whose eyes are always
    Moving,
        Left,
            Right,
                but mainly towards the direction of light.

RUSS RANKIN
Good Riddance

BLANK PAGES

When I stop living
When I am dead
When I no longer walk, talk,
Or breathe
When my insides stop working
Will I leave anything substantial?
Will anything I've done, said,
Or erected
During my brief tour here
Empower, enlighten,
Or endure
When I happen to pause
In the course of an average day
And think these thoughts
It's as if Time itself hits me
On it's way to wherever
It is going
In such a hurry
Why am I?
There are no answers for me
In this life
Only these long days
And blank pages to fill

RUSS RANKIN
Good Riddance

THE FINAL ACT

He balls up both fists
With a single, fluid movement
He knocks himself out
Forever
The pain and bitterness
Like a rabid dog at his heels
All these years
Are gone in an instant
Now the real peace
The final act
In a ballet of despair
No longer will he be forced
To interact with his fellow
Useless husks of skin
Their trite, mundane little dramas
The soap opera that never ends
Until now
No more vain attempts
To attract a woman
Leaving him humiliated
The butt of a cruel,
Biological hoax
The uneasiness lifted
The infirmities of his species
A distant memory
To rot away with the worms
To finally escape
He closes his eyes and,
For the first time in years,
He smiles

RUSS RANKIN
Good Riddance

BUSY?

The barricade is up
And the light techs are busy with the lights
And the sound men
Are working on the sound
And yet I'm still here
On a weathered concrete bench
Inside a musty disco basement
In a crowded Italian city
And the smell is effusive
And the day simply refuses to end

RUSS RANKIN
Good Riddance

BAD GRAFFITI

Two young girls in winter coats
Squatting head to head
Near a crumbling cinder wall
Held together by layers of bad graffiti
With bright blue plastic shovels
They till the fecund soil
And discuss things of worldly import
To a German girl of five
They dig and talk
Talk and dig
On an otherwise barren,
Windswept street

RUSS RANKIN
Good Riddance

THERE ARE THE DOGS

The rare northern sun
Sends a scattered shadow
Across the dew specked grass floor
Of the open air venue
Squatters huddle and smoke
Listening to Discharge
Yes, there are the dogs
The ever present familiars
Of the dedicated anti-socialites
With their pink dreads
And Conflict shirts
Tonight strains of empowerment
Will ring off the graffiti-caked walls
Of this ex-slaughterhouse
While outside you can buy
French fries and cigarettes

AARON BARRETT
Reel Big Fish

UNTITLED WAVE

Tree tops spin
Like elbow water dog balloons
Full figured fandango
I spit into the future and
a cherry flavored dump truck
sits at the opening to the
cave of my misery
What do I see?
The third letter of The
Alphabet

EVAN JEWETT
Maida

EARNEST PSYCHOTICS/PARASITIC IDIOTICS

it is high time for the cutting of ropes
in backwards movies I saw my mistakes
but my heart does not agree with the logically sound
sycophantic ploys to gain entry
into my complicated machinery
while I was caught up in chivalry
you were becoming my circuitry

EVAN JEWETT
Maida

BE KIND

it's always a careless new skirt
and I'm always second best to your visits with sand
a dime for each burden and i'd buy you the answers
fall asleep with your bad habit
breathe it in and hold it
you will never be cold again
i've kept my eyes down
and I've kept my heart shut
but I never forgot
to forget
eject and escape
rewind and erase
eject and escape
rewind and erase

I am choking on your dust

DEREK KIESGEN
Bear vs. Shark

To the credit of the remake
that was a good Dracula
cruel oiled hair
dangerous teeth
fine diction
his strut like rooster
his minion bitches dark sexy

grand two hours
to be the time to leave
to walk down the avenue
with Harker in mind
jealous coward
great gang bowie knife conclusion
retame her
dry up the wet moisture from the lap of the monster luster
fail to see beyond your union and the possibility of a brighter
Harker loose in the pants got his fun
laying tight with the vampire vixens
boobies and inner thigh bites
good job
I hope the marriage to your property lasts forever.

DEREK KIESGEN
Bear vs. Shark

I JUST WATCHED XXX AND IT WAS AWESOME

he jumped barns
he jumped avalanches
he jumped jumps
I kept throwing up and crying because it was so awesome
too awesome
I feel empty now
I feel like dying
I can't ride dirtbikes like him
I can't do that cool sideways thing over a gully
he is an asshole
I am an asshole
there is no reason here
only illusions

DEREK KIESGEN
Bear vs. Shark

They have no tear ducts
just light weight durable alloys
and mysterious gray skin
I would like to four wheel with them someday
trade stories

DEREK KIESGEN
Bear vs. Shark

BENEDICT ARNOLD MIDDLE SCHOOL
Mr. Gregorian

Name:_____
Date:_____

Did you turn in your fitness log?

Exercise	Number of Sets
sit-ups	_____
military presses	_____
bi-lateral warlock crunches	_____
reverse fellated oar benders	_____
Mesozoic chin bayonets	_____
duppers	_____
quasi-yoga thigh lasers	_____
mr. goodtime erection pullers	_____
the egg roll	_____
Mt. Olympus phlangal spear screamers	_____
adult frustration adolescent beauty	
bare-knuckle chalkboard punches	_____
crazed sprint	_____
stern voiced fast food complainers	_____
wasp cloud swats	_____
silent monks	_____
tree of terror	_____
after college is when the doubt sinks in-ers	_____
starforce bacterial nanolevitational	
endoplasmic glute toners	_____
fuck you's and fuck your mom's	
this my classroom	_____
goddammit jump rope routine	_____
push ups	_____

PHIL PIRRONE
A Static Lullaby

No matter what I do, the sun is coming up tomorrow.
Whether it's a good thing or a bad thing.
No matter what you think... what you've been told
isn't scripture and you'll believe what you see
till you're blinded.
You'll think all these things...
No matter what I do, you build these walls to stop me.
It took me years to breakdown the blockade of lies
and if it kills me I'll breakthrough ten million more.
I walk up these steps, but there are locks on all the doors.
The gate is now open, but the bridge is always broken.
Lies are forever spoken, blowing winds of unimportance.
while
bomb-funds are well supported, I stand here....not
informed, not interested, and not listening.

BOB NANNA
Hey Mercedes

Excerpts taken at random from various notes taken on this tour, aka the past 3 weeks:

I wish I could say I've never felt like this. The doors are open now and I am in the van. The iPod is playing Jeff Buckley. Doors are open. And kissing you sucks. Sucks the life out of me. Woke up horribly hot in a cold room. No big surprise. Baby hold my hand. A different interpretation of the obvious. A cop on a horse. My touring. My radios. My waves of love. Go overflow. Let us just be. Almost fatally flawed. Singing saw. Swinging sea. Saw you singing. Flowing baby ribbons play with kittens. That old metallic taste. M'girl. Squeaking hissy tapes. Slight groups of good vibes. We're terribly late for the show. Load-in is now and we're 80 miles out. Good thing I'm not hungry. Pumping some serious idm at the moment. I am unstoppable. Send shovels on the double. Explosions of opinions. Culled culture or whatchamacallit, it still kills o'er the wires. Happy anniversary, stay world famous. Don't be so evil. Sucking down the ink, the cartridge is dark. Blinding bells, showy belly. My young excitable heart speeds faster than any sane racer. Listening up, glistening gills, remembering members, and noir girls. 1234 kids in a line. Good lucking. Many storks ponding, responding, nestled in chicks. Florida for now. Twice the surface noise. A little bit of buzz. A little hiss of interest. A live wire. The Deftones aren't that bad.

BOB NANNA
Hey Mercedes

I'll probably be able to sing tonight. New Orleans may be the hottest, sweatiest, swampiest, most humid dank pit on earth, yet our hooked-up Marriott Courtyard's rooms are Sahara arid. Luckily I came prepared. While the AC was pumping out that dry throat music, my brand new Vicks humidifier was fighting the good fight. You see, a few days ago, a previous humidification product lost and lost big time. Woke up in Pensacola feeling as if I had swallowed a cue ball and it was stuck somewhere between my nose & throat. So that hunk of junk hit the dust fast. And so I hit CVS and found my new hotel roommate. So I'm not 100% but it will do for the show tonight. Provided I follow some ridiculous self-imposed groundrules... I'm assuming we'll be stopping for breakfast soon. Perhaps a Denny's? Perchance an I-Hop? Matters little because here's the deal. I'll order big. I'm going for broke. Breakfast is the biggest meal of the day in this life of a softcore (eggs but no cheese) vegan touring singer. Eggbeaters. Hash browns. Toast, dry (If you don't ask for it dry, you end up getting more butter than toast). Pancakes (Again, I scoop out 98% of the butter they pile on the flapjacks. It should be enough to liberally coat the outside of a Mini Cooper. Don't know why you'd ever want to do that, though.) And of course, that old reliable morning staple, sweet nectar of the gods, lovely java rescue. Now if they don't provide soy milk (or if we haven't squandered it from last night's rider which we get 1 in every 24 shows), I'll gently teardrop some half & half in there. I can't overdo it. Dairy is vocal death round here. Oh yeah, no sugar either. Learn to love it. A dash of butter, a sprinkle of cream, this boy's in the clear, but only in the mornings. Make that breakfast satisfying because it may be the only substantial meal you get today. Now in the van, at gas station number one, I purchase the biggest fucking jug of water they offer. Oddly enough, the gallons are usually much cheaper than the liters. I guess no one wants to be seen guzzling straight from a gallon container. But seriously, who is to judge me here in this van, my home? Todd? I'll shut him up real good when I whoop his achin' aunt fanny in Travel Scrabble! (Plus, when those jugs are empty, they become a handy container for, um, other fluids.) So I have the gallon in hand. if they only have it freezing cold out of the fridge, well then that sucks, but it will have to do. Freezing cold water is vocal death round here. You'll just have to wait for it to be safe to consume. I now have the option of filling up my sturdy thermos with hot water from the side of the station's badcoffeemaker. Today, I'm still getting over Pensacola, so I disassemble three bags of Throat Coat Tea (available from Traditional Medicinals - by the way, TM, i will endorse you for free tea. I practically keep your two-bit company in business!), drop em in and add the hot water. This will steep for at least 20 minutes. After 20 minutes, I'll pour it into a cup and little by little have it burn the hell out of my legs as I try and drink it in a bouncing van. Sort of a masochistic fringe benefit. If things are really grim vocally, maybe grab some throat drops, but for the love of God make sure they're sugar free. If not, you may as well buy a pack of Big League Chew. So the drive. I'll try not to talk too much and never over loud music. Trying to hold a conversation over loud music is vocal death round here. Well what about lunch? It doesn't exist. You get to the club 4 hours before doors so that you can soundcheck. Once you're done, feel free to snack a little on the chips & salsa, the pita & hummos, whatever light they have to offer... because I can't eat a thing at least 3 hours before I start warming up. Undigested food just takes up space & energy when you have more important things to worry about, such as jumping around on a stage. And then, exactly one-hour-before-the-band-before-us-ends, it's time to get down to business. I slink out to the van and get comfortable. I'll hook up the iPod and cue up the 19 minute track known as "Vocal Warmup". It starts with a series of tongue-sticking-way-out "ha ha ha"s. Personally, I don't see what's so funny about being prepared, now listen up. I taped a session I had with a vocal instructor (about 2 months worth of lessons, well worth it, but i think she'd think i'm out of my mind now.) and i sing to her piano. It starts way way down low and some nights I can barely reach it. And slowly it steps up in pitch to way way up high total falsetto. Never ever oversing at this point! This was a problem before. The first day, I told Ms. Vocals that I used to warm up loudly, pretty much in the same manner I played the show. And then she dropped her sandwich. She said that was the worst thing I could have done. So, please take it easy, take it slow. I don't have to tell you that oversinging during warmup is vocal death around here. After the ha ha ha's come the ya ya ya's. And it's the same pitchy routine, this time sans tongue. I believe this exercise was recommended to me in order to combat some wanton orthodontics. Got that jaw click. I also had a cemented retainer removed from my mouth upon her request. My problems must have been major because we go up & down the scale twice! Now while this is happening I take the opportunity to don an ankle brace (old war injury, the battle of grand rapids) and stretch out my legs. Now imagine this. You are walking past a nondescript van and happen to glance over just in time to see some kid furiously mouthing "ya ya ya" for 7 minutes. Do you laugh or run or both? Do you sit and stare in curiosity? After that comes the most embarrassing one of them all. Stick your tongue out. Now say "la ga la ga la" without moving your jaw. Now go up and down the scale. Feel dumb yet? We're only beginning! The la-ga extravaganza is the last thing on the track so turn it off and turn off the van. Now turn on the sirens. I'll start at my lowest possible pitch up to the

highest and then down in one breath if possible, like a police
siren. Try not to force anything. Smooth over that falsetto
break. Get all angelic. Loosen up already, mack. Now go
back into the club. You should have about 20 minutes before
the set change begins. This is the fun part. I'll grab my
Vicks Personal Steam Inhaler (by the way, Vicky, i will
endorse you for free products. I practically keep your two-bit
company in business!), fill er up with water and plug er in to
the nearest backstage outlet. No outlet backstage? Never fear,
just run an extension cord from the stage to the nearest
discreet haven. Hell, during Fairweather's set at Krazyfest, I
plugged into one of their powerstrips and just stood behind
the stage sucking up steam. (Did I mention it was 90+ degrees
outside? Ah, the sacrifices we make.) Sure, you've been
drinking water all day, but now you're moisturizing the
upper regions. The resonant nasal cavity especially (which
right now is plugged like the Hoover Dam, thank you
Pensacola). Suck that steam and suck it good for about 5
minutes (or two Damone / Sensefield songs). Done? Good.
Start stretching. Finish the job you started on your legs.
Then your arms & your back. And finally your neck. I can't
tell you how many mornings I've awakened with "rock neck",
the soreness that comes with headbangin' too hard (I guess it
would happen with shoegazing as well). Then start running
& jumping. It's good to get that heart rate up slowly as
opposed to shocking it senseless on the first note of Boy
Destroyers ifyouknowhatimean. Then you're pretty much
ready. The heart rate is in a good place, the body is stretched
and relaxed, the voice is primed and ready, and you are
totally hydrated from all of that water you drank! You won't
even need any during the show. It's incredible. So phew,
show's over, go talk to the crowd, grab a cold Blatz, hunt
down food, but during all spare time, warm down. You need
to calmly caress your now swollen vocal cords back to their
original size. So make an "eeee" sound, start at a high pitch

and slide down. Eeeeeeasily now, don't force it. When are you done warming down? The answer is: whenever you can speak normally without any gruffness or strain. And there you go. Repeat every day as necessary. Yeah, I'll probably be able to sing tonight. We ended up stopping at a Subway, and then I had to down a Granola bar, I'm almost done with the gallon, and once I get to Houston, I'll need to start working on this nose situation. xxoo bob nanna

AARON PILLAR
The Appleseed Cast
Hundred Hands

in the rain, sing a song, in your head....so secret life, in your eyes, its alright....so be surprised, by the lullabies, that keep us in line, tonight.

THE AUTUMNS

NIGHT MUSIC *

stay
away
from words you can't explain
remember
your reckless father
alone by
the southern waters
two tongues tied two distant skies
flecked with white

last
i heard
two months he'd been in bed
beyond the
brittle urban
ear, feeds
a balmy stifled
air, bleeds
a radio
humming fuzz

girl, you gave me your hand
i know you never had
someone to love you as i have

THE AUTUMNS

LUX *

hey
spare me sweetheartless
the bees
beating their star-littered wings
there where i want you to be

pain
sickly and partial to rain
i'm coming to find you and then
breaking your heart with a grin

stay
who'll explain this?
i'm bled and left under
umbrellas of laughter
someday
you'll be famous
but never forget - it isn't someday yet

stay
there where i want you to be
there where i want you

now
the world
is nothing to see
now and forever
they want you to be
aching to believe

*b-side from the "nocturnes and subades" sessions

RICH BALLING
Cowboy Communist
The Sound of Animals Fighting

JOAN OF ARC DID MORE THAN TALK, JOAN JETT
DID MORE THAN ROCK.

october 10, 1960
an astute, pre-cockney mick jagger
waves goodbye to childhood friend
keith richards, offering his services
to Russia's Marsnik 1 space probe-ram.

earth   mars
~~the rolling stones~~   the rolling stones

God,
help us all.

RICH BALLING
Cowboy Communist
The Sound of Animals Fighting

ALL TOMORROW'S PARTIES

I'll be your mirror,
white light/white heat.
a Sunday morning- the Gift,
the black angel's death song.
I'm waiting for the man, here she comes now-
lady godiva's operation, venus in furs-
a femme fatale.
I heard her call my name, sister ray.
european son, run run run-
there she goes again, heroin.

RICH BALLING
Cowboy Communist
The Sound of Animals Fighting

we are all selfish by nature. some control it better than
others. the biological vehicle for feeling somehow forgot that
choices are made by the chemicals. try. try hard and step on
everyone else to get there. we are all selfish by nature. some
control it better than others. the biological vehicle for feeling
somehow forgot that choices are made by the chemicals. try.
try hard and step on everyone else to get there. we are all
selfish by nature. some control it better than others. the
biological vehicle for feeling somehow forgot that choices are
made by the chemicals. try. try hard and step on everyone
else to get there. we are all selfish by nature.some control it
better than others.the biological vehicle for feeling somehow
forgot that choices are made by the chemicals. try. try hard
and step on everyone else when things begin to look up / S-
U-P-R-I-S-E / time doesn't Stop / and each second
passing Is one second closer to your good streak's End so /
right now i'm trading in a few moments to breathe / and i
hope my Will does not leave me when i choose to exhale /
because that will be the last choice i ever make / i am
restless but / this is the most Comfortable i've been in years /
my mood has shifted from ac/dc to marvin gaye / it's 8:12 in
the evening and / my greatest worry is that i'm missing baby
geniuses Play for a million dollars on Channel 11 we are all
selfish by nature. some control it better than others. the
biological vehicle for feeling somehow forgot that choices are
made by the chemicals. try. try hard and step on everyone
else to get there. we are all selfish by nature. some control it
better than others. the biological vehicle for feeling somehow
forgot that choices are made by the chemicals. try. try hard
and step on everyone else to get there.

ANTHONY GREEN
Saosin

JESUS & THE SHARP, ELECTRIC STAR

Gemüt - Livingston Burgundy
5.99, 2 for 10, we're here
in together anti-vitamin
and the crudest form of nutrient
"you can't hold it against them" she said.
she believes that all those who suffer from
life as from an illness are in the right
the woman in the lobby stares me down
mocking and unconcerned.
In california news anchors all look like
they were plucked from a 3-some porno scene
you've got one hot slutty vixen type
one down from her is the short hot business
woman. in between them is an orange colored 3 piece suit
white haired and 50 something - witty
with a tired dirty smile. the man staying next door
plays his radio just loud enough so you can tell there's
something really close _ _ _ on. When this whole
thing started all i had was a name - now
there's a definition and a reason. the more
i expect, the harder things are.
jesus & the sharp, electric star.

BRANDON BONDEHAGAN
Christiansen

Pop punk takes over
Music in cyclical sense
don't quit your day job

BRANDON BONDEHAGAN
Christiansen

Fallen Oppenheimer Angel
hands his halo back to God.
A naive president waits
for his Latin speaking enemy.
Words with a thousand pictures
of cemeteries, ruins and antiquities.

BRANDON BONDEHAGAN
Christiansen

You'd die to formulate the perfect summer excuse
while dreamin about another girl.
You drive to the point to make out with each other.
Play her a song, brother this one.
Screw until dawn.
And then go on tour.

BRANDON BONDEHAGAN
Christiansen

Thoughts trapped inside the box, concede the dying numbers.
Patterns mold designs. Capsized in time.
A kaleidoscope of styles, inside the cannon fodder
Smashing the shape of things, to criticize.

KENNY VASOLI
The Starting Line

Plane of thought:
Here lay a pensive lettering of my thoughts gathering around
and chatting about ratting out dreams to the conscious
knowing you are waking up soon. With the facts I am given,
and to say that I even know what's going on isn't true, I
could use at least one or two clues before I can get back to
you. But I've got a few questions open for suggestions. Like
what does it mean when a dream just won't leave and you
wake up to face a figment of belief? If I made the corrections
and constant reflections to mistakes I made would a single
thing change? It is strange for me to feel this way? And I
wait... Make lightning strike if the answer is yes! If it's no...
then so be it, but I still want to know who I ask about the
reason behind history repeating itself. Could someone be the
least bit of help?

KENNY VASOLI
The Starting Line

Have a nice life:
I received one kiss for the duration of the trip and it was
loveless as if made by lifeless lips. These lips are sealed you
bitch, so keep that one locked up because it's all that you'll get.
Your life (in my eyes) isn't worth my time on the five-hour
flight. Have a nice life and thank you so kindly for ruining
mine. I hope you and Daniel are living it up, and I hope you
don't miss me and don't give a fuck. Because I'm sure with my
luck this will happen again and someone will replace the
distaste created by the sound of your name. This could be the
last chance I have to elaborate and display the choices I made
and the patiently waiting I did for the day when you'd say that
"my feelings for you are quickly receding, almost as fast as
your heart is beating". When it stops they will stop, when you
drop then I'm off to get on with my life and leave yours with
the ghost of the past.

CHRIS MARTINEZ
Plans For Revenge

IF I HAD TO SAY...

dotted eye's making holes in the skies
winter kiss licking my lips
and i somehow fell into the way
the hair falls in your eyes
the angle of your neck
and sucked into...
your finger tips slide down my face
and all these thoughts i've defined in you.

CHRIS MARTINEZ
Plans For Revenge

BEHIND THE SMILES

the staples in my eyes
the nails in my wings keep me from flying too high
I'm choking on my words
pathetic imitations
surrounding you and I
take my mask and this disguise
I won't try and hide behind all the smiles
my plate is full of knives
biting on the blades and choking on the lies
my wings are made of wax
if the sun burns them away will I fall out of the sky?

CHRIS MARTINEZ
Plans For Revenge

WHEN I DIE

peel the skin off the glass
the blood stains wash away
i still can't remember you
but i do know it's raining
and the black top is bleeding
kill the lights
and sing with the black birds
if i could wear another postcard
and write another letter
you'd all be dead.
all these clouds are grey
i fell asleep with
anesthesia supplements
feathers and voices
this was just the first time.

NICK TORRES
Northstar

I am the cannon that will wreck your home
I am the sword that will reshape your bones
I am the piano that nobody plays
when everybody's home
I know your veins so much better than you
I know the condition of your heart
I can smell the glue
I know where you keep all the diamonds and the meat
I know how to eat them when they shut off the heat
I know the devil
He taught me how to smile
without showing my gums
He taught me which end is shallow

Now I know how fast I gotta run

So keep those pictures on the shelf
And keep your prayers to yourself
We live like this for the laughs, for the fun
And not for God, Not for anyone....
I hear the devil is mixing up some sugar and tea
Round and round with those old rotten feet
So just the basics, no need to poison me please
The bitter the sweeter the better for me

BRANDON PHILLIPS
The Gadjits

ONYX HEART PENDANT

lovers worn
trinkets, charmed gypsy baubles
amber and apron string
by my wrist
arms of silver slither
shark's teeth dangling
apache tears strung upon an anklet.

Pierced and pierced
with silver to kill the wolf
in me jingling like a bird-proofed cat.

cart, pots, pans, beads, rags
brown girls
teaching white girls
drink wine and dance barelegged
satanic string bands
lecherous campfires
lashing tongues and hot taboos.

skills of ten generations
sadly galvanized only by white girls
creating for them
masterworks they
will never stay to see.

BRANDON PHILLIPS
The Gadjits

BODY

torn all asunder pistol-kisser
like tornado blown barn doors
Archibald person on the wall

in the basement of the world seated
omniscient cyclops
daddy-taker
saw all in one deep eye

(the way craters record
ancient rocks
vacuums broken)

ancient blunders
broken vacuums of faith

hope hung up upon
receiver uncradled
no heard dial-tone.

JAMES MUÑOZ
The Bled

BALLADEERHUNTER

this is my nightmare on fuck street.
my codependent collision
near the corner of falsehood and trust.

our beauty,
our tangled wreck,
our masterpiece,
worth endless gazes,

do you believe in the bedpost we're cuffed to
and the mattress in flames?

we're the lovers
with secrets.
and we'll burn in our shame.

JAMES MUÑOZ
The Bled

PILLHEAD CHARRED BY HIS OWN SENSE OF THE SIXTH DIMENSION

blister come hither! relinquish the sinners
who trespassed on greener grass,
traded an ox for an ass,
your wedding day mass;
doused in tourettes
and rung out by bulimics,
your hope will dissolve in a goblet of semen

we raise a toast to our children's prosthetics,
drink up young cynics
your flaws are forgetting,
to mention we baptized our guilty old critics,
in troughs full of carefully pulverized gimmicks

linguists danced with her on plateaus of treason,
waltzing on Neptune's shores,
clogging Octavia's pores,
down on all fours!
sweet sulfur princess (impaled by repulsion)
you wore the tiara like a primetime abortion

we raise a toast to our forgotten believers
the jealous and jaundiced road-rashed deceivers
who left us on empty and up to our necks
in sweet-tooth colonics and model train wreck

JAMES MUÑOZ
The Bled

LITTLE_GONE_LOUDER_ HUNG

so i gave in
and ate five rotten apple cores
from the tree of knowledge
and that
in turn
propelled me thru my memory bank
where i cashed in a gangrened wedding band
for a picture of you
(our anniversary)
being fisted by a diamond dealer,
gnawing the ball-gag with such tenderness,
those tears of joy running down your face,
0 0 0 0 0 0 0 0,
i wish i could give you something so pure,
0 0 0 0 0 0 0 0,
this frame
is faulty
and this
camera's a fake,
sawing off your cuffs,
so sick of dragging dead weight.

ADAM FISHER
Fear Before the March of Flames

dance!answer!bend!swallow!
all hail to the conch(our love)
             dance!answer!bend!swallow!

 rip the flowers from their soil
grab the song bird by its fickle throat
   threaten the sun
                          belittle the moon

this is our dance...there are no survivors

TIM MCILRATH
Rise Against

them's fightin' words

stage set
curtain
song cued
expectation
spotlight
act one
applause, bow
repeat steps

can't you see right now my hands are bleeding?
blisters broken dripping from the ceiling,
I don't want to be here now...
I've fallen apart and I cant pick up the pieces,
I cry in the dark and I cup my ears to seashells,
to hear the solitude they bring...

so many faces, so many voices
so many reasons to give this up
this goes on and on.

can't you hear right now my ears are ringing?
head held in my hands to stop the spinning,
it stops only to start again...
my home has long since been replaced
with a world behind this window pane.

so many faces, so many voices
so many reasons to give this up.
this goes on and on.

have I finally gone too far to come home?
this world might wait for me tonight, but she won't.
now only time will tell if these wax wings will melt,
only moments to spare...

we fall asleep with the color of the sunrise
we count the years on circles under our eyes
we dream in shades of blue and grey...
we speak in tongues of metaphors and stories
we bleed the ink of subtle allegory
we are the needles in the hay...

so many faces, so many voices
so many reasons to give this up.
this goes on and on.

JOSHUA PARTINGTON
Something Corporate

THE DOCTOR'S WAITING ROOM

A plain cream betrayal, hides behind these walls
Distantly voices of referring phone calls,
The nurse seems to say, behind noise-proof glass,
This kid thinks he's different, why should I ask
I almost stood up and walked to the door
But a promise to mother kept my feet on the floor
The hallway was scattered with irrelevant pictures
And cupboards of cures that they swear by like scripture

"Ahead on the left" she said with a smile
I thought to myself this hallway's a mile
I looked for a desk, but saw couches and chairs
And she sat looking at me with the blankest of stares
"So how would you say all the problems started?"
 I looked to the sky as if deeply departed
What an obvious start to an embarrassing tale
Of a life that I loved and couldn't curtail
A family that loved me, an art that I loved
A time that I simply had too much of

"Are you drinking a lot, are you sleeping OK?
It seems like these things could have come into play"
Of course I was anxious to tell her the truth
This had become my family's telephone booth
If I broke down here, what would that mean
Was I not as strong as my father had been?
But I think I can fight this all on my own
With a handful of happiness that never was shown

We talked about writing, we talked about fame,
We talked about why they all called me insane
She talked about being the one that was great
I didn't know much about that, that wasn't my fate
The only truth that ever came out of this mouth
Was a phrase that seems true only after you shout
"I guess I just can't handle the pressure,
I wish I had taken a walk for the summer"

The time winded down and we finished the session
My eyes had been fixed on the clock, it was pleasant,
I left to the waiting room, men waiting for wives
I thought of my friends and their interesting lives
And I stood at the door, the session was done
And I thought to myself, what have I become?

I walked slowly and careful not to cause a big scene
I knew others would be waiting here long after me
Now when I think I had it all on my own
Is now when I realize, I'm really alone.

JOSHUA PARTINGTON
Something Corporate

BURNT VACANT RED

This headache, Incisions,
Machine washed your letters and tore up your pictures
This handle, this feeling
Your hatred: the floor, your love: the ceiling
I wish I, could take it,
All back from saying the lines I was faking

You never noticed
I never said
I'd never need
Burnt Vacant Red

This longing, this tear-eye
I wish I could find you alone on a highway
And tell you, I'm sorry
I cried at your wedding and rained on your party
And if I, don't make it
Feel bad for one moment and after that shake it.

Cause you never told me
And I never said
That I'd never need
Burnt Vacant Red

Remembrance, Sedation,
A plane ticket home and a life of frustration
A gift horse, to glance at,
Thrown away food for beggars to stare at
I'm broken, I'm Tired,

I still miss the times when I was inspired
I'll never tell you
What's all in my head
And pity me hiding

Burnt Vacant Red

Intentions, Submissions,
An analog clock compromised my position
The Fragile, The dagger
Still on broken glass I drunkenly stagger
The Voices, inside me
Are stand-alone fixtures and reasons for hiding

And I never showed you
When we went to bed,
That this heart in my chest,
Is Burnt Vacant Red

NATE RUESS
The Format

ON YOUR PORCH...

i was on your porch
the smoke sank into my skin
so i came inside to be with you
and we talked all night
about everything you could imagine
cause come the morning ill be gone

and as our eyes start to close
i turn to you and i let you know

that i love you

well my dad was sick
and my mom she cared for him
her love it nursed him back to life
while me i ran
i couldnt even look at him
for fear id have to say goodbye

and as i start to leave
he grabs me by the shoulder and he tells me

"whats left to lose
 youve done enough
 and if you fail well then you fail but not too us
 cause these last three years
 i know theyve been hard
 but now its time to get out of this desert and into the sun
 even if its alone"

so now here i sit
in a hotel off of sunset
my thoughts bounce off of sams guitar
and thats the way its been
ever since we were kids
but now, now weve got something to prove

and i, i can see their eyes
so tell me something, can they see mine?

cause whats left to lose
ive done enough
and if i fail well then i fail but i gave it a shot
and these last three years, i know theyve been hard
but now its time to get out of this desert and into the sun
even if its alone

i was on your porch last nite
the smoke it sank into my skin

MARC MCKNIGHT
Nightfall

...WITH JEALOUSY HIDDEN IN THE SOIL

There are many signs
as slowly it comes.
Furnaces shine gold on three cities!
The dead are burning now.
From the east the sun is rising.
Faultless and idle, Men stand in the dusk.
Leaning heavily on the abandoned .

From the enemy we defend
Armless race with the winds
Night burials leave dawn to empty streets
Children are dying!
And we're scattered among the shelter of marriage.

These walls fall as fast as tears
With years of waiting for the sky
To shine its gold on this city.
So much hate comes from thirst
A taste of water seems hollow!
These cities are buried with starvation

The sun stands on the sky
While our roofs give in to the wind
These houses are flooded with wonder
Of how a man could drown
A life from opposition.
Follow.
Shout!
Give and run with arousal

A chance to see the murderer(ed)
Fight to stay alive.

MARC MCKNIGHT
Nightfall

MAKE MISERABLE AND CAUSE SORROW IN OTHERS

Mistakes are often fatal,
But a good beginning is half the battle.
And a good, practical commencement
Is a Pledge, a promise
Satisfied with resolutions of well doing
Enjoy the fruits of the industry.

Search lights.
Or light on dark corners.
Find the power in words
Cause for every faker
there are a hundred enemies.

There are few crimes beyond a loss of character.
Maybe a degradation of reputation
Who shall repair the injury?
Who can redeem the lost?
What person can heal a ruined remedy?
Warn the people that contact implies death.

Self Control.
Self control means courage in a foreign form
Support of a character can be found in habit
And in habit one can find the root of all virtue.

revenge is a Poor creature, crawling through life

Fame never magnifies character!

And well ended
is half begun

JASON GLEASON
Further Seems Forever

THIS IS NOT ME

what's it like to make a metaphor?
my mother's a womb
my dad's a guitar
my love is a heart
or a kiss
or a star
or a prayer for my life as I sleep in the car
she's a doctorate in rain
and the same last name
or a light in the dark and my god is the same
my life is a speck of dust
or a flame
and I'm all the better for it
not knowing, or caring, it's not for me to choose
some call it trust
some call it faith
it's all just a matter of taste
and this is not me
and I've fooled you all again

JASON GLEASON
Further Seems Forever

catching the grayest of blue skies when
love is just too big to know
straddling april's winter when the
heart is only half whole
for pouring myself onto misguided streets
that I turn
and traffic will always be waiting for me to catch up,
to catch up,
to crash,
to burn
oh exit, exit, she calls out my name
catching her breath on my memory stained
I remember a time when I traveled afloat
but my ship has a hole...
and it's only a matter of time till I know

JASON GLEASON
Further Seems Forever

1+1=3 (REASSURANCE)

white
green
white
green
white
green green green green...
red, always seeing red
amore Divino.
don't let me fall
two white wings and I know you won't let me fall
pt. 2-
and I never would
but just know while we sleep
He'll be holding us up
for the world
kind of like flying
kind of like floating
something like swimming in the womb
but it's just me and you and 1+1=3.

CHRIS HAYNIE

WEAR AND TEAR.

There is an empty house six miles down the road filled with
nothing and soggy walls and floor beams that ache and ache
from not being walked on in so long and they would creak and
creak if they could, if only someone would come up the front
steps and give them a good battering or stomping or stamping
or maybe just a soft dance whether there was music or not and
oh how the walls wanted music. The house was an empty place
filled with nothing not evens of all sorts, nothing not evens like
wine and shoes and gushy, smiling children who peed on the
floor at night because the bogeyman was outside, and nothing,
not even air, and if there had been things inside they would
have floated like birds, but there was nothing inside and even
if there had been it wouldn't have mattered because there
wasn't even light to see it with, and oh how the walls wanted
light, because they were painted such a beautiful color.

MARK THOMAS KLUEPFEL
The Reunion Show

my entire life is a really bad b-rated 80's movie; not like "Earth Girls Are Easy," but like "Monster Squad"

MARK THOMAS KLUEPFEL
The Reunion Show

Technology will kill me,
So will poor penmanship
(and spelling and grammar,
well and also logic)

JAMISON COVINGTON
JamisonParker

I wish that I could claim these words as my own, but they've
come from someone that understands this world far better
than I could ever imagine. In a time of disposable love and
faith based upon circumstance, a time where we'd rather
watch someone else's life broadcast on our television than
take part in our own triumphs & tragedies, a time where I
know that I'm not the only one that has a need that no
prescription or product can even begin to fulfill.......I'll
never claim to have any of the answers, only the same
questions as everyone else. Take joy in being ignorant with
me, for ignorance is bliss. I was once told that what separates
intelligence and genius is realizing how little you really know
& what separates faith and blindness is a thing called hope.

ROBERT MONROE
Maida

his ocean wrists run deep.
but the floods before him,
will not be cause
to drown.

JOSEPH TROY
RxBandits

T&R&K

I took a bulb and crushed it with my foot. I was wearing
shoes. The thin glass did not penetrate. If it did, I may not
have even felt it. Besides, a bottle of brown poison had taken
over most of my blood cells. Still, I break my legs as I break
contact with you. If it's hours I wouldn't know. It's just time
and we cannot pull it off with any valid amount. Chain me to
you, so no time can separate us. Visit with me forever, or
contemplate crushing the same bulb beneath your bare feet.
You need to feel it. This will become easier or harder and I
choose the latter. But I need your chain, even though its links
are broken.

JOSEPH TROY
RxBandits

...PERIODS...

My barstool breaks from under me and I find the ground is
far more idealistic. The glass shards tear into my arms, legs
and stomach, leaving me to bleed. Letting me suffer.
Watching me hunt for an answer. I'll tell you my secret:
There was no stool to start with and I've lain in glass all of
my life. I give myself the pleasure of blood to experience how
you felt as you drug your hands through your own period.
Your sickness is revolting. But still I watch from the ground
and roll over and over on my impending body and soul. I
watch you as you stare into the red curtain and hope that you
become one with it. I stare into your eyes and wish to become
one with you. Fucking my blood with yours, making this
blood combination.

JOSEPH TROY
RxBandits

WHAT WILL IT TAKE TO RUIN YOUR DAY?

This fire is burning. The light it provided yesterday still
hangs low in your room. Smoldering lamp feeds sickness to
your blood. The bird sits on your windowsill, Mocking (as it
should), your eyes that have been dissolved by the heat. She
smells your disapproval and makes it worse by defecating atop
anything you wish to remain pure. Ha ha. Blind and filth
tattered. I never want to know you or how you feel knowing
me. Because then I would have no choice but to throw my few
senses into the smoldering fire and fuck what I have become.

JOSEPH TROY
RxBandits

DIVIDED SHADOW

Detached but still self-centered, I could be lying down or
standing up. Both ways I would feel warm next to you. The
sky omits nothing. No light, no stars, no moon. All founda-
tions of purity and innocence can be divided by your touch.
Still, restlessness overcomes all and defeats no one but me. A
shadow twist of faith can be seen and heard. With all else
silent which noise can be recognized? For I do not understand
the true meaning of this shadow. It is temperamental and dis-
obedient. I wait for light to lift it away as if it were a nullified
illusion. Please be an illusion.

JOSEPH TROY
RxBandits

I CONTROL YOU I CONTROL THE VIEW

At this point, there may be no turning back. As if the
halfway point only existed as an awful excuse for tears: I'm
drowning in this rented water... Your's. Each breath continues to drive me to drink this death. Lawless and lost. Fucked
with fusion. Physical and permanent. Bashful and betrayed.
Tortured and motherfucking demolished. This wrecking ball
strikes all that lives in peace to make your world survive in
my bitter delight. This wrecking ball will fuck your world and
I can control it. If you want to fight back, find your own
fucking disaster.

JOSEPH TROY
RxBandits

PENN TO PENN

What the fuck happened to the last one home? She swore she
would be the first. Payments for her subtleties were not worth
the wait. As her life continued, her eyes bled more and her
throat remained forever dry. I can watch her die before me; I
can watch myself die as well. Will this last? As you arrive I
will perfect my departure. Depending on the final destina-
tion, your call might not be received and your face will have a
hollow hint of yellow. Don't trust the mirror, though, that
will only make it worse. Don't trust the puddle of water, the
fountain or the glass. They are all liars and as I watch you
come home I will be one for you. Your comfort zone parallels
my boredom.

JOEY CAPE
Lagwagon

THE ARMS RACE OF SOUND (LULLABY)

Waging war on the arms race of sound
Turn it down Pull the plug
Imminent surrender Ringing in the new Dark Age
Shut down the noise-aholics
Put down the quiet-ophobics
In a daydream of peace
In a calmness too brief
My lullaby is killing
My lullaby be stilling
It could be such sweet silence
From static from violence from...
Volume is the modern currency
Everyone competing for airspace
Everybody's dumb
Shouting muddled words as though they're Deaf
Big brother isn't watching anymore
He knows we are distracted and absorbed
Broadcasting our grief
Our imaginations atrophied
We can't think
If I could sing them all to sleep
If I could sing myself Deaf
Wouldn't it be lovely?
Doesn't it sound perfect?
Every generation hates the next
I will save the millions from a slow insufferable death
I'll put them to sleep
Save them from progressive misery
I'm counting
If I could sing myself to sleep
If I could sing myself deaf
Wouldn't it be lovely?
Doesn't it sound perfect?
My lullaby is killing
My lullaby be stilling
Memorized involuntary
I think I can change the world

GARED O'DONNELL
PlanesMistakenForStars

A BELLY FULL OF HELL

it crept to me like a cancer in my sleep. it gnawed the meat
right from these bones. and so it seems somewhere, somehow
the wonder was stolen and the truths we held were squandered or sold. and these walls will find us beggars, liars and
whores. it's getting colder quicker, and we're putting bets on
who's quickest to leave. we picked our poison, talked shit, but
couldn't choke it down. we tapped the vein. we tainted the
trust. this silver spoon has been licked to rust. if this were a
test we'd be failing it!!!!!!!!!!!!!!

STEVE SCAVO
The Color Turning

AS THE HEART DEPARTS
All my friends they each will tell you different things
but it's the comfort that kills me
Art you said was more of an obscurity
It was you
and you're right where you should be
you're doing nothing
amidst applause
your heart is empty
your judgment's pending
Left alone to your devices
it's hard to say that this would be better
that this would be sane
This life is mine
What's your intentions?
If that was as good as it gets
it's just enough to forget
If that was as good as it gets
it's just enough to continue again
I know your face
I've smelled your waste
I've seen your heart
And I can't look again
For my reflection's just as dark
If this is the last breath I should take
I'm just getting better
"In life we learn from our mistakes"
I'm married to mine
Take all the things you've left behind
they've haunted me always
and here's to years and years of smiles
if only forever

JUSTIN PIERRE
Motion City Soundtrack

IT'S HARD TO BE SPONTANEOUS AND KICKASS...

every once and awhile however, I have what's known as a
"bright idea". but, very rarely do I ever make it happen. "in
the head" is always better than "written down" and "written
down" is always better than "on television". but, it's so easy
to flip the switch, turn the dial, sit down and kick one back.
(it should be noted that "kicking back" often gets in the way
of the "bright idea"). perhaps, that's just the way of the
"bright idea". perhaps that's just in my case. perhaps not.
either way my "bright ideas" rarely see the "light of day" and
no, that was not meant to be a reference to michael j. fox, but
I can see how one might draw that conclusion. that said,
spontaneity is so very important. yet, had it not been for the
likes of raymond chandler, russell banks, neil gaiman, elmore
leonard, phillip k. dick and woody allen, to name a few I may
not have developed as quick a wit as some believe me to
possess. little do they know, I still require the assistance of a
dictionary to look up the big ones.
(written between the hours of 9:21pm. and 9:31pm. in toronto,
ontario on october 10th 2003 in the basement of the
kathedral)

JON ORISON
Oris

HADES' SHADE

I woke up with a feverish pitch piercing my hidden mind.
Sweat dripping in slow beads from my helpless fear,
Guarding my sorrow through a wind blown night,
I felt a knock at a door unused in years.
A fence of tears mounted a barricade around movement,
Held in position to remember her.
To touch her uneven eyes with no candle light,
A dark trek into an unforeseen life,
No control and no sight,
Emotions played without ploys,
Only quiet tries,
Yelling whispers to the lonely night—-I love her.
Will she ever know?

Frozen souls become melting snow,
Riding down avenues with pictures of old beliefs.
People forgotten but still seen,
Killing love,
Killing everything!
Unholy witness to a dying dream.
And me,
Alone to hold the blame,
In a desert home left to feel her shame,
Old conversations chase her away.
The magical (four),
Out of (seven) he stays,
Holds her at present,
Not afraid to watch the young woman fade.
Wants her in elder years,
Wants her beyond the past,
Wants her to be the last,
To change with the young man!
To bathe with the young man!

Walking into holy lakes never seen,
The heart has nightmares of a lovers dream.
This one he needs may rest uneasy,
The wounds she feels spill into this night.
He could not sleep again in places she's been,
Reaching through the air to touch empty sin,
To touch something to defend.
Will this woman love him?
Or will he rest uneasy in a shadow parade,
Left to burn slow in an edited frame,
Pleasure is a show to a past filled with pain,
His heart cannot live as a link in her chain!

The sorrow would push him to Hades' shade,
Can't talk to the others,
Can't make them go away.
So he walks with the struggle-
Love brings a new day.

Erin, my heart hurt last night...

JON ORISON
Oris

MAKE LOVE TO GOOD FRIENDS

I want to pretend,
Shake hands with ambassadors,
Make love to good friends,
Trade revenge to open ends.
Cut cards with the holy ghost,
Eat stems off the Lotus tree,
Toast to life till I can focus!
A beautiful world hovers before us.
Come touch and gel with truth,
So free others are invisible to meeeeee,
I walk through them to bring peace and relief.
A lonely soldier to rally the dream,
Cast spell with a whisper,
Turn tricks in the hall,
Let men touch my body,
Let women have a ball.
Walk tightropes smoking cigarettes,
Grab others as they fall.
Remind them of beauty and a short night of lust,
Trust no one to listen.
You are love dipped in blood,
Drip on mouths of stone.
Form taste on their tongues,
Put love in their lungs,
Unleash passion from trees,
Dance naked in the breeze,
When I feel you I feel peace.

CHRIS SHEETS
RxBandits

HAPPY BIRTHDAY

You followed me home as a means to an end
and promised but one thing to which you could lend
        who wants to be the one that we all see?
So happy, set free, bent over so cheaply on a knee
widespread, the trouble lies inside, but far too deep
mindsets, the voyeur released just outside of me
        who wants to be the one that we all see?
Reaching the summit and setting thoughts free
excursions to perversions, salt the earth like the sea
loosing it all in a gripped free-for-all
don't know you but you show me every night to the fall
whispering words and they don't mean a thing
it's that look in your eye that keeps bringing me in
Skin's crawling away, and my love, so are you
up, out, and over my interest now subdued
purging myself in the filth of your body
lending itself from the tame to the gaudy
The sun will soon be up and strike us down where we lay
shade the only testament to a game zealously played hung out
and flayed makes the unfolding obscene taking delight in
agony we lick each other clean.

JASON CRUZ
Strung Out

NYLON

She is the last verse in a thousand bitter love songs,
Torn from paper sung into void.
She's the last call when I ain't even numb yet.
She's a creepin' flame up my leg,
When all I wanted was a warm night
Alone.
She comes just when I need her to,
But never knows when to
Quit
She calls herself the apocalypse to my new red hope,
Yet she offers no misfortune
When she shows up at my door.
She's everything and everywhere I look-
In lipstick smeared suicide pumps-
Watching in silent gaze
At the matchstick boy
Ablaze.

JASON CRUZ
Strung Out

PERSEPHONE

You're the illusion of purpose.
Blindly and rhythmically enhancing the destruction of all,
You motivate the will and mortify the senses.
You're the Jesus in the eyes of a fanatic, pushing your
madness to fruitation.
You're the broken heart in the chest of a fool, lovesick to
Suicidal grace.
You hide your meaning in the eyes of the dead and laugh at
the sane.
You're the trigger happy lunatic aiming at the only mirror
you haven't shattered yet,
 You're my best friend.
You're the music that leads the blind over mountains and off
cliffs,
And you know no end.
So here I wait,
Because you know I will.

JASON CRUZ
Strung Out

AMBULANCE CRASH

HERE I SIT,
LOOK AT ME.
A CASUALTY OF MY ENDLESS SUCCESSION
OF NEEDS AND DESIRES,
ESCAPING ONLY FOR A MOMENT TO DEVOUR
WHATEVER LOST SOUL
FEEDS ITS MOMENTUM INTO THIS,
GLASS MACHINE.
WRITE A LITTLE LOUDER
AND THE WORLD MIGHT HEAR YOUR BULLSHIT,
TALK A LITTLE SWEETER,
AND THEY MIGHT CARE.
YOU SEE IT'S AN EASY WORLD OUT THERE,
IF YOU'RE JUST LOOKIN FOR A CAR CRASH TO
ADMIRE
THAT IS.
TWISTED STEEL AND BROKEN BONE BECOME THE
ART
OF A DAMNED MIND,
SO COOL YOUR EXPRESSION TO HIDE YOUR LUST
FOR ANOTHER EYEFULL OF SOMEONE ELSE'S
UNLUCKY
SIDE SHOW.
YES,
LIFE IS JUST ONE RUN-ON SENTENCE
AND I CAN GO ON AND ON AND ON...
BUT I WON'T.......
UNLESS YOU'RE BUYIN'!

DERRICK W. SHERMAN
The Reunion Show

I once met a man and asked him if it were true that when you get older you become wiser. He said that the only answer was to get older. Looking back to when I was a kid, I realize that my ignorance was a virtue. I saw the world in colors and shapes. Now my nerves keep me awake at night. I think about the future and what I want to do with my life. I asked that same man if he had any advice for me. He told me to quit living and start breathing. "Look around at the life you lead. Listen to the wind and the trees. Take time to smell the ocean breeze and sleep on the beach." He said that the beauty of this world was in its complexity and that our lives for the most part are ordinary. He told me to never stop painting, but mostly never stop creating. "You're as free as your mind will let you be. So, what's holding you back?" he asked, "fear or laziness??"

ANDY HERMES
The Junior Revolution

Convictions come out through your eyes
Pouring out your dark rimmed, empty glasses

We try to sit and try not to talk
Both waiting until this moment passes

Fishing for feelings as you drive like a ghost
You say I'm a wreck, I feel like a car crash in quotes

TIM ELSEY
The Junior Revolution

-] SELF FULFILLING PROPHECY [-

We live in a world, where we search for meaning until our
hearts stop beating
We mostly search for ourselves
But what we find may be deceiving
Lost in cryptic meanings
When we look inside our souls

Some say we can't help who we become
It's the fault of society of dad, and mom
What you reap is what you sow
Who you become is up to you

We are the products of ourselves
We are the products of self
We are the answers for
Questions worth asking
We are the products of ourselves

All in due time, all in due time for me
All in due time, all in due time for me

Ask yourself, what is real and what is not
Find yourself, unable to tell the difference
Save yourself, but not at the cost of losing others
Save yourself, from me

We are the answers for
We are the answers for
We are the answers for
We are the answers for

We are the products of ourselves
We are the products of ourselves
We are the products of ourselves
We are the products of ourselves

MIKE ELLIOTT
Blue Sky Mile

STAY IN BETWEEN THE CHANNEL MARKERS

Stretching out his arms,
as if on, suspension of
the pulpit during swells;
he
with heave and say integrity tried to life preserver others that
he
did not know intimately, yet the reality
of those overboard, now under burdened;
provoked
this good samaritan to see focally, farther
less than the buoy.

MIKE ELLIOTT
Blue Sky Mile

USING BOTH HANDS TO COUNT

jenny any choir, would stand, staring down,
swaying side to side, as if unimpressed
by the chorus, on altar, claiming their
song as a cause for praise,
pitch, and scream.

hands at her side, following her cloth design,
dressily singing on note and in key as
effortless and unarduous as all kids
will be while listening, yet again, to
unheard of melodies.

peaking above the pew line of fine, submerged
behind blank eyes, i could see this was all
more of a damn fantasy achieving
vitality in the limits of pursuit
without the boredom.

her protest is the best one that comes to mind, for
she no longer can find solace with hands clasped
together, interwoven, showing the place, and yes
its steeple, but for all that's inside, there are not
as many people.

MIKE ELLIOTT
Blue Sky Mile

CHRIST I PAID TOO MUCH MONEY FOR THAT TRIP TO EUROPE

this snow bends branches back
and lays still with a gentle breeze
on these mountain peaks

night contends with distant candle flames
and it lights more suns seen than the day
in this wilderness

a lake, almost frozen,
paved the reflection of the sky above me,
below me as well, with symmetry

on the ground, shadows cast
silhouettes in the snow
away from the heavens

voices air with little orbit
and kindle, as fires,
the strength to keep warm

while sledding the deep dark alps,
all the stars i've never seen
but four of them, drifting, fade

is it these visibilities
under this winter solstice
that caption a new moon?

KEITH GOODWIN
Days Away

CALL IT WHAT YOU WANT

I went from ok to now. Not knowing that this is not what I
care about. Thinking I'm right. If I move faster I will pass
out. I'm feeling lucky that my hands aren't still tied down (to
me pushing myself around). This is the worst and I still
complain. It would make sense not to feel the same way for
days. Mixed drinks for the girl and grey. More of a reason
for me to stay. Too soon. More time for myself to lose
(interest). I'm in this now and then. A bad mood that never
ends (quickly).

MATT EMBREE
RxBandits

I tear for the pauper's quote, the invalid's letter,
misguided and misdirected, buried in insecurity amidst
the piles of discarded dreams, landscapes and memories.
He who commands the unthinkable from the depths of
inhumanity,
the rot and the filth and the undeniable urges stuffed in
bowels
and stinking, putrid and disgusting.
Those who lust for the disaffected and pipe for the terror
of wide-eyes and bleeded hearts. The heat proximity in their
temples and their loins, all erect and function, squirm
and fail.
From moon and sun, through castanet claps overheard the
rhythms,
hips thrown forth like hades' ember and molten sex.
The come of a thousand, shrieking for the closest moment
to death, the clearest mind-state, the almost touch of
reflection
daunting and powerful the feeling through guts.
They who sew light together with whispering wands and
antelope
leaves, thirsting for a vacation from this reality, to turn in
this past and sever their aortas.
Who fling themselves naked, bored, restrained and helpless
into
the pits of despair so they may find a way out.
They who shoot poison into their lungs and suck saliva from
the mouths of the listless and beaten down. Fresh to your
grave
I commend thee.

MATT EMBREE
RxBandits

It's nice to see you all here with your uniforms on
black on black on black
studs on spikes on silver
posthumously clapping for the wind, trying to chase it as it's
changing erratically
mocking laughs
winding up to throw gestures into full size mirrors
and cry as they shatter, beautifully
In a dream I picked up a shard and ran it across my wrist
The blood ran down my forearm and dripped from my elbow
they all complained
It was making a mess they said and went on to agree that it
was better when they all stood in a circle, backs to the world
alright with me they said
It's so nice to see you here, now with your cotton confections
and witty interjections they intersect to complete
I am going to take off my clothes and bleed to death in the
corner
for I haven't the faintest about chases anyhow.

MATT EMBREE
RxBandits

Take all the murder with you
for now we are saved
But you know as well as I that I will tumble
once and a million times again
and I'll walk in circles, mumbling inaudibly
Maybe I was singing those words for you
only to let you die
with my arm outstretched
like moving lines in a Japanese cartoon
these roads forgive like the souls of the dead
conquered by technology and blonde hair
much like we walk through the streets
with our eyes closed tightly we block out the sound
the grating within our hearts
it grows light with antiseptic
a healthy dose of falsity to the cranial of society
and our OH SO beauties
who walk the streets in the hippest style
with fashion in their hip pockets
I've got the flask
the love, the burn, the icicle wand
I'll give you the kiss from the shadows
and the scimitar to the belly
we'll stroll that catwalk together baby
painted and rearing to blow.......

MATT EMBREE
RxBandits

How many poppies to fill that voice?
How many angels to kiss those lips?
How many strangers to woo and cuddle under the same stars
running the gauntlet like thieves high on freedom and
sensory lust
The kings of the road, the buffalo of the concrete jungle,
the semi truck diesel burners of the atlantic ocean, too salty
and
dry like morning after sex, crusty and smelling of razor clam
still hip on last nights drunken fumbles tracing thigh veins
and operatic crevice treasure. The miles of time, the soprano
strings, flat at first but climbing to the top. Add to stir
an evangelizing head rush all tip and little shaft. Lick lipped
liability in tremolo and infinity. How long till the blood is
dry on her satin, salty and thick like when my lips curve to
reveal my orthodental sacrifice.

BRIAN MARTINEZ

Dear Ginsberg...

I wrote a letter to Ginsberg and
and sent it to the sky,
through my eyes and to the
nearest stars and with pupils
opened wide, I cried and cried,
unashamed, uninhibited. the
angels read aloud to Ginsberg,
sitting in some heavenness sky,

I proclaimed,
Oh Ginsberg you made me weep
and weep the teary-est tears
for all my years, although
only twenty, I aged with you
and sat in my skin
rocking and creaking
like nana's old rocking chair.

And a soft chuckle,
short gasps of breath
that otherwise would have
been the screams of
beauty like some lonely
streetlight that begs
to be stood under,
orange skinned
and orange tinged...

And to here you sacrifice
yourself time and time again
and splattered your bloody
ink and your invisible
soul to me and to others
and I wiped my eyes once
again..

I proclaim oh Ginsberg,
you made me wish for a soft body,
and soft hair,
naked touches,
and the power of the nail
that scratches and marks
the skin and be handled
and and and and,
for the cool soft sweat
and shivers under the covers...

You made me want to
jump off balconies and
out of windows testing the limits
of constructed worlds
and falsehoods that look
like movie sets,
and find the rubber air bags
to catch me,
and say ha! I knew it!

Ginsberg,
I apologize for stealing
your style,
I promise I'm not
making a dime...

Ginsberg,
how I am suppose to
write what you have already
wrote? How will I see
everything anew,
and fresh,
will they come to me?
Or will I have to dig
under the graves of dead
plants, dead water
to see a reflection,
a simile,
a verse?

No wait,
Ginsberg,
don't tell,
don't kiss,
don't, kiss and tell,
stay silent,
I don't want to know,
I want to know,
but I want to know...
I'll know
when I see it,
when I feel it,
when I smell it,
and when I do, I'll weep
for me,
weep for you,
weep for the world,
weep for everything imaginable,
weep for dusty roads,
and highways,
weep for new clouds,
and new adventures,
weep for weep,
weep for weep's sake.
for this I will sleep and wake.

Dear Ginsberg, thank you.

SCOTT GROSS
From Autumn to Ashes

MALE HOOKER IN A BATHTUB

Ok, so it's a blind chemical machine I'm dealing with here in the
frontal temporal lobes of grades 1-4. Your parents thought you
were ok until they found you hanging from the doorknob. You're only
four feet tall and that's a long enough dick to slip into
the holes in the palms of my hands. Have faith in nothing
or you'll believe in everything. I believe the receptor when we
fuck. We fuck to songs that have no rhythm and that's why I'm
so in love with you. I'm so in love that if you turned your back I'd
claw your fucking spine away. I'll never sleep with medical junkie book
reading whores. You're the perfect whore. I'm losing my ability to do the
only thing I know how to do and as the nights are longer I know I must
take myself as easily as possible, and I'm not taking you with me.
So the stairs are my up and I crawl and I crawl and I sit in the bathtub
because the acoustics are better. I hope my mom and my dad are proud.
I hope they understand how much I hurt. No water. That copper hit the
linoleum and I released before it all fell to my shoulder. Maybe someone
cared.

JARED DRAUGHON
Classic Case

DOWN AND OUT

My time spent yesterday,
trying to control the way that life would lead me in has
somehow failed.
Now all I do is try to find my way out of endless possibilities of
doubt.

My time spent today,
fighting to remedy all my mistakes has brought more problems
then before.
Still I try to find my way out of endless possibilities of doubt.

I've been down and I've been out from time to time and in
between.
I've been sure that I've had doubts of all the truths that seem
to be.

My time spent tomorrow,
will be uselessly hoping to eliminate the inevitable.
I'm sure I'll be trying to find my way out of endless possibilities
of doubt.

I've been down and I've been out from time to time and in
between.
I've been with; I've been without all of the things I seem to
need.

If I keep this pace then I risk everything.
Now this overview of solitude has been reviewed.

I've been down and I've been out.
I've been sure that I've had doubts.
I've been with; I've been without.
I've been down and out.

JARED DRAUGHON
Classic Case

SATURATED

I will sail until the ocean brings me closer to a land that welcomes me.

Soon the tide will rise and wash away the island where I'll die a cast away.

Meet me down by the water.
Don't believe in the calm before the storm.
My mind is saturated by the rain that keeps leaking indoors.

The flood will fill the atmosphere; I'll stay onboard until the coast is clear.

Meet me down in the water.
Don't believe in the calm before the storm.
My mind is saturated by the rain that keeps leaking indoors.

Hurricanes seem to stare me down while drowning me.
Now the air evaporates into water everyday.
All the clouds gather rain as they drift toward me insisting that they won't quit till I'm washed away.

Meet me down underwater.
Don't believe in the calm before the storm.
My mind is saturated by the rain that keeps leaking indoors.

ANDREW LOW
The Jazz June

I LOVE NEW YORK IN FEBRUARY

"There is a class that controls a country that is stupid
and does not realize anything and never can.
That is why we have this war." – Ernest Hemmingway A
Farewell to Arms

There's a sting in the air
like breathing too much aerosol
The comrades are restless
with blank stares they learned in boot camp

Your eyes are loose teeth
teething on insides
Poorly drawn war paint
runs in hot tears
evaporating in the steam of the sewers

Concession stands can't keep up with crowds
forming on 5th Ave.
Stomping for a recount
and a quick camera angle
Acute like the bend of the arm

The poetic nature of real life sprayed in gas clouds
tossed by brick through windows
The highly political nature of the length the underarms
sits side stage
as bomb threat sirens ring from the bus station

PS 101 is out of session this afternoon
due to paper towel rolls disguised as pipe bombs
Kids on lock-down pick gum off the bottom of their desks
with fluorescent rulers
that state Murphy's Law of, "What ever can go wrong, will."

A game of Contra is on pause
in the subways of 42nd street
Grey snakes whip through concrete arches
bringing white power donuts to the attention of train
attendees

"They shot down our space ship!" rang through the station
this morning
The mourners navigate through early morning congestion
saluting our flag in an attempt at courage
while outside ducking from crop planes slung low

This wave of filth takes a deep breath, hiccups and coughs
filling the sewers with Rats' blood
Tonight will be fair warning
and oak tag banners
hung loosely over shoulders

"Let Freedom ring! Lord God all mighty let freedom ring!"
In our ears as we sleep
and digress
Till the wave breaks and salts this bare sunrise

REVOLUTION

117

ALEX HOVIS
Who Killed Alex?

I'm sorry I never hurt you more than this
My door is shut and your lies will never make it out alive
And I am sorry that I am disturbing
I just find sorrow interesting
I'm pining over you and I really don't know why
Because I could never look at you
Without wanting to bruise your pretty face
And watch you cry with mascara on my fist

ALEX HOVIS
Who Killed Alex?

I will never forget the way you looked sitting next to me
And how you smiled while we rolled around on the ground
But soon we were alone and it was time to learn your taste
And kiss your lips and grab your waist and feel your hips
Late nights have never been the same
And your words a week later could have killed
But when your heart is gone it sinks into the skin

JESSE KURVINK
Hellogoodbye

THE SOUNDTRACK TO THE SUMMER.

so i guess that this is the soundtrack to the summer? you've been sick since april which is about how long i've known you. lately you've been staying over because you can't bring yourself to go home and you say you don't remember what it's like to be more or less content with your life. well, here's a little jogger for your memory if you can't quite recall the countless nights we stayed awake trying to forget about the fall: we were sitting in my room, not getting tired after two a.m. we were listening to "the wild, the innocent, and the e street shuffle". we were sitting up in bed and i was playing with your hair and you said "the summer isn't over yet but i feel like the trees are already dead" and i said "maybe that's just something inside of you that's been blooming and dying for years", and you left with my sweatshirt like you always did, loudly out my front door and quietly into your side one. and when i finally convinced you to come back out i took you for a walk and we talked about all the things i'd been afraid to say for the last six months. do you remember now? well, do you?

JEFF DAVIS
Boys Night Out

THE LONGEST LAST CALL

It's last call at the hospital.
You slept through it all, and these four walls warn you that your surgery might not be the key to fix your memory of you and me.
Last call at the Hospital, emergency room is drowning in alcohol.
The empty halls, and empty chair means you're all alone and no one cares.
You see that flickering exit sign above the entrance to the morgue, and you can't wheel your stretcher fast enough. I see the flickering behind your eyes and your bloody beacons are begging for pulled plugs and empty sockets.
I traded arteries for batteries to keep you living through the winter, drained your blood and pulled out splinters, sat back and watched the curtain close and screamed applause to an empty crematorium.

EMERGENCY

Seized, interpreted, re-organized, and plagiarized with permission and encouragement from "Days of War Nights of Love."

Think about your direct bodily experience in life.
No one can lie to you about that.

How many hours a day do you spend in front of a television screen? A computer screen? Behind an automobile screen? What are you being screened from? How much of your life comes at you through a screen, vicariously while you sit and watch. Is watching things as exciting as doing things? Do you have enough time to do all the things you want to? Do you even have enough energy to?
Do you think for yourself, independently, or do you take others' word for truth? How often do you find yourself repeating something you heard another say without it having any bearing on you personal experience; your personal truth? How many hours a day do you sleep? How are you affected by standardized time, designed solely to synchronize your movements with those of billions of other people? How long do you go without knowing what time it is? Who or what controls YOUR minutes and hours? The minutes and hours that add up to your life.
How do you feel in large crowds of anonymous masses? Do you find yourself blocking your emotional responses to other human beings? Can you put a value on a beautiful day? How many dollars an hour salary does it take to stay inside and sell things or file papers for someone else? What will you get later that will make up for this day of your life? How many days have you given to such things?(years?!?)

Do you have ideas or do ideas have you?

Who prepares your meals? Do you ever eat by yourself? Do you ever eat standing up? How much do you know about what you eat and where it comes from? Do you trust it? Of our many time and labor saving devices, do you find yourself with more time or ironically less than ever? Is it even possible to "save" time?

They're buying your happiness from you

Steal it back
How are you affected by being moved around in prescribed paths, in elevators, buses, subways, highways and sidewalks?

By moving, living and working in two- and three-dimensional grids? How are you affected by being organized, immobilized, and scheduled...instead of wandering, roaming freely and spontaneously? How much freedom of movement do you have-freedom to move through space, to move as far as you want, in new and unexplored directions?

How often are you waiting? Waiting in line, waiting in traffic, waiting to eat, waiting for the bus, waiting for the bathroom--learning to punish, ignore and control your spontaneous urges? How do you feel when you suppress your desires, when you delay or deny yourself pleasure?

Do you ever need to be around nature? Have water, leaves, foliage, and animals been replaced by your pet, aquarium, and houseplants?

Do videotapes of yourself and your friends fascinate you, as if somehow you are more real in image then in life? Would a movie about your life be interesting? How do feel about the non-stop barrage of audio, visual, print, billboard, computer, radio, and robotic voices that guide you through a forest of advertisements? What do they want from you?

How often does your happiness come in conjunction with buying something?

Do you feel like without the mainstream stimuli that you will miss something? Will you? Does it make you tired reacting all the time instead of thinking on your own? When was your last true moment of silence...not white noise but pure silence?

Have you ever asked yourself these things?
Do you feel violent impulses?
Do you feel inexorably lonely?
Are you really happy?
Do you ever feel like you are going to lose control?

Do you have the energy to create change?

CHRISTOPHER ZERBY
Helicopter Helicopter

I'LL KILL YOU IF YOU DON'T COME BACK

Howland, shirtless, walks slowly in the heat toward the liquor store that seems to shimmer in the distance. People are everywhere: standing on the steps of the beat-up houses that crouch too closely together on either side of the street, hanging out of windows, and sitting on the green wooden benches in front of the bus stop. Others drive by anonymously. Howland steps around two small, caramel-colored girls drawing pictures on the sidewalk with chalk, crooked rectangles and squashed circles. He stops. One of the children shades her eyes and looks up at him, squinting against the sun.

"What's that?" Howland asks.

"That's our money," she says. The other girl nods. Then they bend their heads back to their drawings, kneeling on the pavement in baggy shorts and tank tops.

That must hurt, thinks Howland, imagining their tiny, skinny knees scraped up, raw and painful, pebbles sticking to the sore spots. The girls are around the same age as Howland's daughter, Tina. He hasn't seen her, or his wife, in at least a month.

Howland wipes beads of sweat from his bald head with a shaky hand, and wonders, briefly, when he first started going to get his drinks when it was still light out and there was so much of the day left to get through. When he looks at himself in the mirror, he doesn't see a guy who drinks every day, who needs to drink. What he sees isn't so hot though— it's a guy who looks older than Howland thinks he should.

*

Inside the liquor store, several things are happening. First: Sandeep is changing the tape in the cash register. It's a pain in the ass. The machine whirs and kerchunks as he holds one end of the paper delicately between his fingers while the other end is fed into its slot. Second: Mrs. Tilson is taking a six-pack of Bud Light out of the beer cooler in the back, the same thing she gets every day. Third: a kid who Sandeep thinks he has seen in the neighborhood is standing at the end of the whiskey aisle, alternately looking at the beer cooler and Mrs. Tilson's large, sunburned breasts, straining at her white halter top.

*

Howland stops again to light a cigarette. There's no breeze, there hasn't been any in days and his underwear sticks to his ass and bunches between his cheeks. He looks around to see if anyone is paying attention, and picks at it, annoyed that small things like that, dirty things, require his attention. He begins moving again, his white belly jiggling in rhythm with his walk; ten years ago he might have cared, might have been ashamed of it. But not now, not in this neighborhood. Gradually over the years, Howland has felt his center of gravity move ever downward. He remembers reading how men are balanced at the shoulders and women at the hips, and as he ambles down the sidewalk, he feels his haunches sway to counterbalance the weight of his stomach, and he thinks, fuck this; it's not really fair.

*

Mrs. Tilson smiles at Sandeep as she places the six-pack on the counter. Sandeep frowns back. He has no time for this big white woman who is in his store almost every day. They all show up more or less every day. Sandeep doesn't drink. When he has no customers he spends his time working over the crossword puzzles in the Globe, learning words like "gala" (a big bash) and "rill" (a small stream). I speak better English than most of these people, he thinks. In the round fish-eye mirror, he watches the boy as he opens the door to the cooler, shuts it, opens it again. He has on camouflage pants and a gray sweatshirt. It always amazes Sandeep that the neighborhood kids think they can buy beer from him with their pathetic fake I.D.s

Mrs. Tilson hands Sandeep a five-dollar bill. He snaps shut the plastic case that covers the register tape, pops open the drawer with the push of a button, and takes the money.

*

Howland can't believe how hot it is. He wishes for his Ford Ranger, useless and rusting out, the transmission shot to shit, now parked at the curb in front of his apartment building. The fuckers wanted $800 for a rebuilt job with fifty thousand miles on it. No Goddamn way. But the truck could take him out of the city, up to Gloucester maybe. He could spend the day at the beach. He could get some fried clams and eat them outside at a picnic table, drink a Corona with a lime and watch kids run around with their mothers in pursuit. Young mothers hopefully, in bikini tops with towels wrapped around their waists. He is sure he has been to a place like that before with Tina and his wife. He has done those things, but it seems like a long time ago, even though it's not. Lately, all those memories seem fuzzy. Two boys blow past him on the sidewalk on a bike, one furiously pumping the pedals, the other sitting on the handlebars. The bike wobbles and tilts from side to side as they struggle to maintain their course. No mother chases after them.

*

Sandeep watches Mrs. Tilson make her way toward the exit of the liquor store, one hand holding the six-pack, the other scratching at her thigh, causing her shorts to ride up, just enough so that he can see the beginning of the generous curve of one ass cheek. Maybe she's not so bad. She pushes the door open and exits, allowing the sound of passing cars to enter for a moment before it swings shut. Sandeep looks for the kid and spots him in the mirror again. He stares intently after Mrs. Tilson, then opens the cooler and pulls out a forty of Old English. Okay, thinks Sandeep. You want the beer. I would take your money if I could.

*

Up ahead, on the sidewalk coming toward him, Howland can see Mrs. Tilson, unmistakable with her dyed red hair. And her breasts. She lives across the street from Howland, and he knows her old man Bill is long gone, everyone knows, it's no secret in the neighborhood. He picked up and left about six months ago, walking out one night with a bag in his hand, slipping on the icy pavement, and struggling to step over the snow bank that had been pushed three feet deep along the sides of the road by the plows. Mrs. Tilson, Anne, screamed at him as he opened the door of his Buick and threw the bag on the passenger seat. Howland had seen and heard it all from his second-floor window. Now he waves at her as she comes closer and she smiles and gives him a nod. What the Hell had she been yelling at her husband that night? Howland can't quite remember.

*

Sandeep watches the kid walking up the whiskey aisle

toward the register. Keep coming, he thinks, keep on coming. You won't get that beer. No way you're more than seventeen. The kid approaches. He has a fuzzy red mustache and zits on both cheeks. He takes small quick steps. He glances behind himself several times. "Furtive," thinks Sandeep. "Surreptitious."

*

"Hey Anne," says Howland stopping on the sidewalk and throwing his smoke into the street.

"Hello," she says. She kicks at the ground with one sandaled foot. Drops of water bead on her bottles of Bud Light. She looks up at Howland, looks him in the eye. Howland tries hard not to stare at her breasts, at the dark spots of her nipples, which he can just make out under her top. No bra.

"Jesus," he says. "This weather is going to kill me."

"Can I bum a cigarette off you?"

"Sure. Yeah." Howland reaches into the front pocket of his cut-offs and pulls out his slightly crushed pack of Marlboros. He hands her one and lights it for her. She looks all right. She must have been pretty great a few years ago.

"I would buy a pack, but I don't want the boys to see me smoking in the house. You know."

"Yeah. No need for them to see it in their own home."

"How's work?" she asks.

"It's good. It's work." Howland works nights as a security guard in the local Foodmaster. He stands around smoking cigarettes by the entrance while the stockers roll huge pallets of groceries up and down the aisles. Most of them aren't big talkers; some of them don't even speak English. Sometimes Howland just shows up, punches his card, and gets through his whole shift without saying anything to anyone at all.

He can feel sweat running down his bare back. He remembers Mrs. Tilson standing on her step yelling at her husband, hugging herself in the cold as he'd driven away. She had kept on yelling even when the car was way down the road. When Howland had left his wife she hadn't yelled, she hadn't said anything at all. She had just sat there on the couch watching the news, her feet up on the coffee table, the remote in her hand. Tina was at her grandmother's when it happened, where she had been spending more and more time. When Howland thinks of that night, he likes to picture his wife upset, in tears. She grabs him by the shirt and he shakes his head, sad for them both, sad for his daughter, but sure he's doing the right thing. He pushes her away gently, and as he goes out the door she's calling after him, "We can make it right, don't go." But he does.

*

Sandeep has definitely seen the kid hanging around the neighborhood. He doesn't know whose kid he is, but Sandeep doesn't like how he looks. He guesses the kid doesn't like him either, his brown skin, a lot of them don't. It could have been this kid yelling out the window of that car the other night, "Sand Nigger!" That one's not in the puzzles. The kid puts the Forty on the counter.
Sandeep glares down at him. "You got I.D.?" he asks.
The kid just stares back, his arms crossed. His hands shake a little.
Sandeep leans forward on the counter. "No I.D., no beer," he says. "Got it?"

*

Blasting a Latin pop song out of an open window, a car passes by Howland and Mrs. Tilson as they stand on the sidewalk. Howland knows that Bill was some sort of carpenter, or construction worker. He was a little younger than Howland, a big guy, but in shape, and he had some sort of tattoo on his bicep, a fading black and green symbol, but Howland can't remember exactly. Howland can see Mrs. Tilson's dark roots, her real hair, about an inch or so before the red starts. She has to be thirty-five, thirty-six.

"Well, hey," she says. "I gotta get back. Thanks for the smoke."

"O.K. No problem. I'll see you around then."

"Right. Have a good one."

She edges past him on the sidewalk. Howland watches as she goes by, her thighs white and smooth in the bright sun. She's all right, he thinks. He tries to remember the last time he got laid, but he can't.

*

The kid reaches into his sweatshirt. He pulls out a pistol and jams it into Sandeep's neck. The silver of the gun contrasts with his smooth brown skin. Sandeep half expects the kid to say something clever, like in a movie. How's this for I.D.? But he says nothing. Sandeep longs for his own gun, which is sitting next to the safe at knee level. I never should have leaned forward, he thinks. That was a stupid, stupid mistake. The kid pushes the gun harder into Sandeep's neck, forcing his head to the side, and grabs him by the hair.

"The register," he says.

*

"Hey Anne!" Howland calls.

Mrs. Tilson stops and turns to look at him.

Howland has no memories of her before the night her

husband left. Surely, he's had some sort of interaction with her--a nod in the street, a hello at the corner store. He had known Bill, at least in passing. They would always stop and talk Red Sox when they bumped into each other. But the first memory he has is of her standing there, yelling as the car drives away.

"What?" she asks. She holds the six-pack on her slightly cocked hip.

"We should get a drink sometime," he says. "If you feel like it."

Mrs. Tilson shrugs. "Yeah, maybe. I'll see you." She turns and continues walking down the sidewalk. Howland scratches his belly. He wishes he were wearing a shirt. He needs some beer to get him through the worst of the heat, and then later he'll need something a bit stronger. He shuts his eyes tight and tilts his head toward the sky. The sun burns bright yellow through his closed lids, and it feels very heavy and makes him very tired. It's hard to do things when it's like this, he thinks. It saps your strength.

*

"The register," the kid says again. He pulls Sandeep's hair tighter in his fist.

Sandeep reaches over awkwardly. The kid is pulling his head in one direction and the register is in the other. Sandeep's fingers glide over the buttons, knowing each and every one by size and position, like Braille. Then he finds the right one, hits it, and the drawer pops open. He pulls bills out of their slots, first the ones, then the fives, then the tens, and places them on the counter. But no twenties. Sandeep puts the twenties through the slit in the time-release safe underneath the register. He takes no chances.

The kid releases his hair and regards the money. The gun is still pressed into Sandeep's neck. The kid grabs a handful of cash and shows it to Sandeep. "What the fuck is this?" He drops the money and takes Sandeep by the hair again, this time pulling his head down, across the counter, until they are face to face. The kid's eyes are drab and brown, and his pupils are huge, blown way out of proportion as if he were trying to see in a dark room. His breath smells of what? Corn flakes? Sandeep wonders if the kid can smell his breath, and if he can recognize the yogurt he has eaten earlier, if it is sweet, or foul, or not remarkable at all. He's surprised he's not shaking.

"Is this all?" asks the kid. "Is this it?"

Sandeep nods. The safe won't open for hours, there's nothing he can do. He's going to die at the hands of a stupid kid, a fucking white kid, probably too stupid to hold down a job. So stupid that he robs a liquor store in own neighborhood where lots of people are sure to know who he is.

"They'll know it was you," says Sandeep. For a second, Sandeep thinks he sees understanding in the kid's expression.

"Shut up," says the kid. He brings the pistol up and then swings it hard down on Sandeep's head.

Sandeep slides to the floor behind the register, catching a blurred view of the kid picking up the small bills and stuffing them in his pants pocket. O.K., thinks Sandeep. That's O.K. He sees his own gun sitting there next to the safe, resting beside his crossword. How about that gun? That's going to be big surprise, I bet. He reaches for it, but his arm feels too heavy. It must weigh as much as that safe, he thinks. Instead he picks up the crossword, about half-filled in. "Stagnant" intersects with "Misapprehend."

"Bitch." The kid is peering over the counter at Sandeep on the floor. He puts his gun back into his sweatshirt and picks up the forty of Old English. He turns and walks toward the exit.

Sandeep hears his footsteps on the linoleum. He can just

see the fish-eye mirror from his spot on the floor, but he can't find the kid in it. He sees rows of bottles distorted in the reflective surface, blown up like brown bowling pins, and the ghosts of colored lights from the neon signs on the windows of his store. I wish I had that gun, he thinks.

*

Howland kicks a Coke can as he walks through the liquor store parking lot. A couple of steps, kick. A few more steps, kick. What had Mrs. Tilson been yelling that time? Howland knows he'll go to work that night, stand outside the Foodmaster, and everything will be quiet, and he'll think, just as he always does. He'll replay the day's events in his mind, and he'll wonder what his wife is doing, who she's with, what's going on in her head. Is she fucking that guy from work, that Rodney? Maybe some other guy in her office, some guy who had probably been sniffing around just waiting for Howland to leave, waiting for an opening, a chance to move in. He kicks the Coke can. Has Tina seen it? Does she know what's going on?

A kid comes out of the liquor store with a forty-ounce beer. He's skinny. He glances once at Howland and turning sharply to the right, hurries down the street. Howland watches him go; he looks familiar. That red hair, those camouflage pants--not a likely combination. A neighborhood kid. How could they be selling him beer?

Howland hurries to the entrance of the liquor store and shoves the door open. He sees no one, no customers, no one behind the register. The Pakistani guy who is always there—always—he's missing. Howland pants in the air-conditioned store. His chest heaves. In the reflection of the cooler glass, in the fluorescent lights, his belly looks whiter, paler than ever.

"Hey!"

Nobody answers. Howland's fists are clenched and raised.

"Hey! Somebody better answer me! You can't sell beer to children!"

The liquor store is silent.

"Goddamn it! Somebody has to answer!" Howland pumps his arms helplessly.

*

In the fish-eye mirror the fat man looks funny, distorted. "Indistinct"? Wasn't that a clue? Sandeep raises his head to look for his crossword and sees it in his hand, rolled up in a tube. Now, just give me a pencil, he thinks, and I will write it in.

"Sometimes a scream is better than a thesis."
                                                    - Ralph Waldo Emerson

REVOLUTION

vomit forth the hare from shells

, long since abandoned by the snail,

while the hinged   ches

exhales no breath, for , unlike his unwitting   companio

he has not forgotton the
                        approaching
air balloons

John Gourley
Anatomy of a Ghost

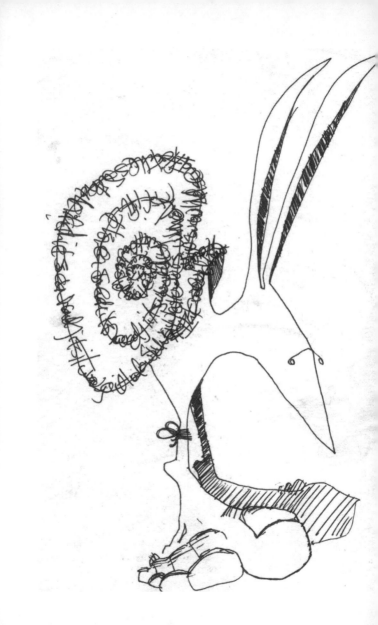

John Gourley
Anatomy of a Ghost

John Gourley
Anatomy of a Ghost

Chris Tsagakis
Rx Bandits

REVOLUTION

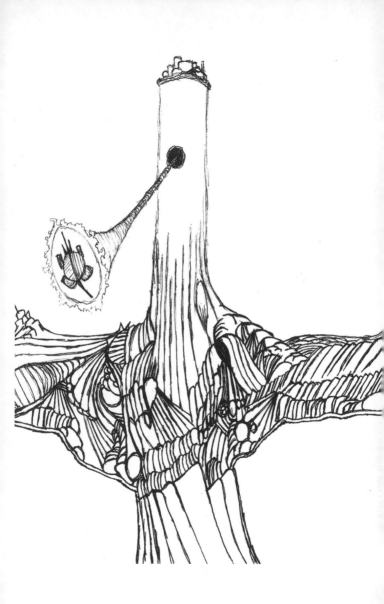

this is the DNA structure for a creature who would've existed had its DNA not been so complex and unorganized at the same time. Evolution weeded this creature out of existence, despite its potential for supreme intelligence.

Chris Tsagakis
Rx Bandits

REVOLUTION

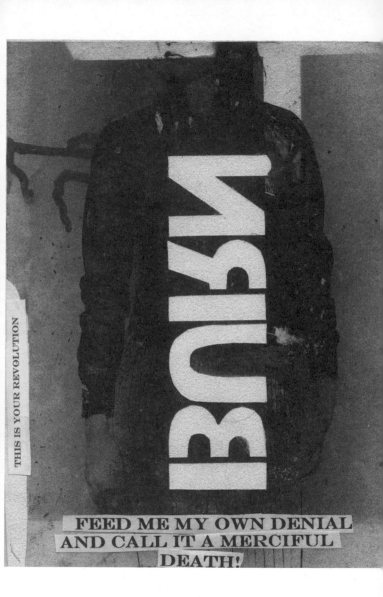

THIS IS YOUR REVOLUTION

BUSH

FEED ME MY OWN DENIAL
AND CALL IT A MERCIFUL
DEATH!

148

Jason Cruz
Strung Out

Jason Cruz
Strung Out

REVOLUTION

KEEP THE
HEART
PUMPING;

RISE

LOAD YOUR
HEAD

CREATE
A NEW
DISORDER!

Jason Cruz
Strung Out

REVOLUTION

Chris Hughes
Moneen

Chris Hughes
Moneen

REVOLUTION

ARTIST CONTACT / INFO:

Dan Arnold
www.astaticlullaby.com

The Autumns
www.theautumns.com

Rich Balling
www.cowboycommunist.com

Nate Barcalow
www.finchmusic.com

Aaron Barrett
www.reelbigfish.com

William E. Beckett
www.theacademyrock.com

Brandon Bondehagan
www.christiansenonline.com

Mike Burkett
www.nofxofficialwebsite.com

Joey Cape
www.lagwagon.com

Jamison Covington
www.jamisonparker.com

Jason Cruz
www.strung-out.com

Bobby Darling
www.gatsbysamericandream.com

Jeff Davis
www.boysnightout.com

Jared Draughon
www.classiccase.net

Mike Elliott
www.blueskymile.com

Tim Elsey
www.juniorrevolution.com

Matt Embree
www.rxbandits.com

Adam Fisher
www.marchofflames.com

Colin Frangicetto
www.thisdayforward.com

Jason Gleason
www.furtherseemsforever.com

Keith Goodwin
www.daysaway.net

John Gourley
www.anatomyofaghost.net

Anthony Green
www.saosin.com

Scott Gross
www.fromautumntoashes.com

Chris Haynie
www.adastrabooks.com

Andy Hermes
www.juniorrevolution.com

Alex Hovis
www.whokilledalex.com

Chris Hughes
www.moneen.com

Evan Jewett
www.killmaida.com

Joseph Karam
www.thelocust.com

Derek Kiesgen
www.bearvsshark.com

Mark Thomas Kluepfel
www.thereunionshow.com

Jesse Kurvink
www.hellogoodbye.net

Andrew Low
www.geocities.com/the_jazzjune/

Brian Martinez
drummer979@aol.com

Chris Martinez
www.plansforrevenge.com

Tim McIlrath
www.riseagainst.com

Marc McKnight
www.nightfallca.com

Robert Monroe
www.killmaida.com

James Muñoz
www.thebled.net

Bob Nanna
www.heymercedes.com

Jonathon Newby
www.braziltheband.com

Gared O'Donnell
www.pmfs.net

Jon Orison
www.orismusic.com

Joshua Partington
www.somethingcorporate.com

Brandon Phillips
www.thegadjits.com

Justin Pierre
www.motioncitysoundtrack.com

Aaron Pillar
www.theappleseedcast.com

Phil Pirrone
www.astaticlullaby.com

Russ Rankin
www.good-riddance.com

Vincent Reyes
http://go.to/fitm

Matt Rubano
www.takingbacksunday.com

Nate Ruess
www.theformat.com

Gabe Saporta
www.midtownrock.com

Steve Scavo
www.thecolorturning.com

Chris Sheets
www.rxbandits.com

Derrick W. Sherman
www.thereunionshow.com

Jeremy Talley
www.thebled.net

Jarrod Taylor
www.inreverentfear.com

Shane Told
www.silversteinmusic.com

Nick Torres
www.isthisthingloaded.com

Joseph Troy
www.rxbandits.com

Chris Tsagakis
www.rxbandits.com

Kenny Vasoli
www.thestartinglinerock.com

Christopher Zerby
www.helicopterhelicopter.com

"The universe is made of stories, not atoms."
                                        - Muriel Rukeyser

AD ASTRA RECOMMENDED READING LIST:

The Girl in the Flammable Skirt, Aimee Bender

Hot Water Music, Charles Bukowski

Invisible Cities, Italo Calvino

If on a Winter's Night a Traveler, Italo Calvino

The Fall, Albert Camus

The Stranger, Albert Camus

Waiting For the Barbarians, JM Coetzee

Notes From the Underground, Fyodor Dostoyevsky

The Complete Plays, Sarah Kane

On the Road, Jack Kerouac

'Till We Have Faces, C.S. Lewis

The Life Force Poems, Gerald Locklin

Captain's Verses, Pablo Neruda

The Complete Stories, Flannery O'Connor

1984, George Orwell

Cannery Row, John Steinbeck

The Mysterious Stranger, Mark Twain

IV. DEAD CHRISTMAS

A selection from "The Honey Ditch" by Chris Haynie, coming Summer of 2004 from Ad Astra Books

About a million and a half years ago when I was in school and worrying about the ins and outs of every little path to the promised land, I used to walk home with this girl for cookies and TV. So goddamned cold on those half miles home, a thousand days of warm doorways and rationed pop. But I guess you know how cold doesn't matter one fucking bit when there's someone like her.

That's how it all works, falling in love with a million coincidences, hoping that you're not just noticing these things now.

Praying for rainy days so her mom would invite you in "until it lets up", and in her bedroom, grasping over damp clothes, saying things to her slow so they would sound eight times more profound and a million times brilliant.

I never believed in God and she never believed in showing up late to church, and it made me wonder what was wrong with second best.

I respected her for believing in God the way she did.

But Sundays could get lonely when there were only your own damp clothes hugging you.

I'd go out to the woods on those days, looking up to the treetops and shooting the shit with myself. Sneaking up slow behind bushes to keep from scaring deer. They heard me and kssh ksssh and away they went.

My dad took us out there a lot when I was young, but I had to take myself out there when I got older because he started spending afternoons with Jim Beam.

I took her out there on some Sunday, after much persuasion and hand grabbing, and showed her the same places he had shown me a million and half years before when I was ten.

And so we stumbled through the woods, slow-walking at first, then breaking into a full run to pretend-escape the rain, we fell down and we picked each other up, and again the rain saturated our clothes and we collapsed on the ground and looked up to the sky and watched the rain fall on us. We were a million and a half miles away from everything and stupid and naive and falling in love with each other and every second. The weather was furious with us. And it let us know with a fresh torrent and we abandoned our landing and made our way deeper into the woods as one last protest to Sunday deadlines.

We found a river a few hundred feet later and we stopped at the ledge above it and I said:

"Say hello to the river Carrie!"

"Say 'hello'!"

And we slid down the embankment and managed to make it about half-way across before it was up to our pockets and we turned back. We discovered we had been betrayed by our senses during our descent, and saw something we hadn't seen in the embankment on our way down, about 15 feet of box-shaped decaying planks enveloped by the mud.

It spurred something in my memory and I remembered my dad taking me out here on a just terrible cold day, and the snow was beating down on us as we looked for dry wood for the kiln, and it had gotten so rough, just so cold.

And he said, "It'll clear up, just wait."

So we did and it didn't, and we spent more than a few hours gathering wood waiting for it to finish up.

"This isn't going to work."

He lit a cigarette and I remember being out there with him and watching the smoke make its way past his face as we walked fast to nowhere searching for a place to take some refuge from the snow.

It was getting heavier and colder and the snow was keeping us from moving and I had never seen him so close to giving up on anything before.

"There it is..." he said, laughing to himself.

" The goddamned honey ditch, I knew it was out here somewhere."

We looked at the structure and she grabbed my hand. The building, a telling gray-green now from a hundred years of snow, barely resembled what it was when my grandfather built it. My grandfather, a carpenter, was also a beekeeper of all things. As it was a thing of those post-depression years to keep a side-job like Roosevelt told you to.

"Keep yourself moving Davie." he told me on some dead Christmas.

"Keep yourself moving because there's always someone catching up with you."

How much gravity that might have had was negated by the aftershave of that coarse man, overpowering and skewing an eight-year-old's perception of the future or the future's responsibilities.

We made our way to the foot of the embankment and scurried up the ledge, making our way to the mud-effaced structure. I ran my hands over the decayed wood and it was a hundred years ago again.

*

And my dad was telling me to tie the rest of the wood together while he looked for the door. I took off my gloves to lace the twine in and out of the wood and the cold burned me pretty bad and, it was real tough to concentrate and I kept looking up to see if he had managed to get in the door yet.

*

And so there we were, frantically searching the same wood to cajole an opening. After a few minutes of digging mud away from flaking paint and pine, we found a boarded entrance and the nails gave way to our prying. And I looked at her and motioned for her to go first and she smiled back at me and pushed me through the door.

*

He had found the door under snow and black leaves, and we crouched inside and managed to close the door behind us and he took out the flashlight and the lights came on.

*

We searched the cabin, through old boxes where the bees were kept and found some matches and got an oil lamp going and talked about the rain and her life outside of the woods and she pinned me on the floor and kissed me, and a thread of light caught her hair and for a second all I could see was auburn sunshine.

*

"Your grandpa used to spend whole damned summer out here, smoking these bees and jarring. And he'd bring me out here sometimes, and we'd wash out in the river afterward."

He offered me a cigarette, and I took it because a feeling somewhere between diplomacy and longing told me to, and I stomached the smoke and coughed out choppy clouds in response to his drawn out inhales and graceful exhales.

*

I touched her hair and we rolled on the damp wood floor and fumbled for each other and the cold of the rain encased us in the room and she took off her shirt and I didn't know what the hell to do so I took off mine and Christ we were only 15 and I kissed her a little longer and we put our jackets over us and slept.

We woke up and the one string of light creeping through the doorway had crept down to our feet and she saw me looking at the door and pulled my head back towards her face.

"I love you Davie."